INTRODUCTION

Every year, organizations across
hundreds of billions of dollars
But it's blindingly obvious that the standard and quality of leadership in the world today is woefully inadequate. Something isn't connecting. All that investment isn't making a dent in the problem.

I'm not a theorist (although I consider myself to be a student of the human condition). I built my career without the luxury of being an expert in any particular field. My executive career took me across many different industries and job families, each new role thrusting me into an unfamiliar environment in which I had no choice but to give up or engage.

I've seen all kinds of major organizational change: mergers and acquisitions, geographical expansions, corporate restructurings, IPOs, joint ventures, and asset disposals. These experiences gave me deep insight into what really drives leadership, culture, and business performance.

I also learned very quickly that I possessed some core skills that are transferrable to any context: communication, negotiation, decision-making, influencing, and relationship-building. But what propelled me more than anything else was my ability to get results through others; to unlock the latent potential of my people to achieve extraordinary outcomes.

My upbringing instilled in me a sense of higher purpose, the desire to pursue excellence, and a fundamental belief in doing what's right, not what's easy. My mother was a woman of incredible selflessness and humility, a small measure of which I'd like to think rubbed off on me. She had an acute sense of fairness, and put others' interests ahead of her own, sometimes to her detriment.

I was incredibly fortunate to be educated at one of Sydney's leading private schools, which proudly bears the Latin motto *In Meliora Contende*—"Strive for better things." This was not about the acquisition of material wealth, but rather the obligation that each of us implicitly has to improve our part of the world, however big or small. We were taught to set noble goals, dig deep to find courage and bravery, focus on the greater good, and never succumb to complacency or mediocrity.

It would be disingenuous, though, to suggest that I've always lived up to those ideals. There was a period in my early adult life when I departed from these values for several years, as I experimented with my identity. Although it was a lot of fun at the time, it ultimately brought me no joy. I learned through trial and error that I'm actually happiest when I adhere to the discipline of strong principles and ethics.

Throughout my leadership career, this knowledge has been more valuable than I can possibly describe.

These unshakable ideals have driven me to attack my greatest fears, head straight for the most difficult challenges, and ignore conventional wisdom. I'm wired to go against the usual, and that enables me to venture where most leaders wouldn't dare to go. This has opened up vast opportunity to discover the underlying leadership behaviors and competencies that genuinely make a difference.

The leadership development industry is dominated by academics and consultants, many of whom have never experi-

NO BULLSH!T LEADERSHIP

MARTIN G. MOORE

RosettaBooks®

No Bullsh!t Leadership

Copyright © 2021 by Martin G. Moore

First edition published 2021 by RosettaBooks

Cover design by Mimi Bark
Interior design by Alexia Garaventa

ISBN-13 (print): 978-1-9481-2278-8
ISBN-13 (ebook): 978-0-7953-5308-6

Library of Congress Cataloging-in-Publication Data:
Name: Moore, Martin G., author.
Title: No bullsh!t leadership / Martin G. Moore.
Description: First edition. | New York : RosettaBooks, [2021]
Identifiers: LCCN 2021018900 (print) | LCCN 2021018901 (ebook)
ISBN 9781948122788 (hardcover) | ISBN 9780795353086 (ebook)
Subjects: LCSH: Leadership.
Classification: LCC HD57.7 .M644 2021 (print) | LCC HD57.7 (ebook)
DDC 658.4/092—dc23

www.RosettaBooks.com
Printed in Canada

RosettaBooks®

YOUR
CEO
MENTOR

To every leader with the courage to be better

"For the simplicity that lies this side of complexity,
I would not give a fig, but for the simplicity that lies on the
other side of complexity, I would give my life."

—Oliver Wendell Holmes Sr.

CONTENTS

enced the stark reality of leadership in the trenches. They've never faced the gut-wrenching dilemmas leaders are often presented with when making difficult decisions.

They've never had to tell a young mother with three children, a large mortgage, and an unemployed husband that she no longer has a job. They've never had to make a decision that could make or break a business in a highly ambiguous and rapidly evolving world. They've never had to muster the strength of character required to lead people through a crisis. They've never had to change the culture of a legacy business to establish a higher standard of behavior and performance. They've never had to master the discipline required to let go of control and let their people perform at their peak.

I have.

What I've captured in these pages is the accumulated wisdom of a person, very much like you, who simply chose to make a difference as a leader, and has the scars to show for it.

That's what makes this book unique. It's based upon my real-life experiences and practical wisdom gleaned on my journey from law school dropout to CEO of a major energy business with a track record for delivering real performance uplift over a sustained period. //

STRONG LEADERSHIP IS TIMELESS

Leadership has never been more difficult. The new world we find ourselves in has brought us *face-to-face* with the fragility of our circumstances, our economies, our livelihoods, our longevity, and some of our most prized freedoms. Yep, there's nothing like a global pandemic to focus the attention.

Many leaders have floundered through the *COVID-19* crisis because they were unprepared. And I don't mean unprepared simply in terms of business continuity planning, although that's virtually a given. I'm specifically referring to their lack of resilience, their inability to function in a highly ambiguous environment, and their unwillingness to make decisions at the necessary speed. In other words, their inability to do the things that great leaders do.

Although the pandemic has shone a spotlight on these shortcomings, what constituted great leadership before still defines great leadership today, and will remain the yardstick for great leadership well into the future. The principles are timeless, if we can only understand what lies at the foundation of strong leadership: *To strip away the bullshit and lead.*

In times gone by, it was a lot easier to get away with poor leadership. The *command-and-control* leadership style that many of our parents experienced was predicated on rigid organizational hierarchy, *co-location* of people, and sustainability of employment.

Try that style with a Millennial, in the gig economy, who's working remotely... Good luck with that!

This book unlocks the secrets of great leadership by cutting through the clutter, the platitudes, and the uplifting rhetoric to get to the things that really matter. *What type of person do you need to be to lead others effectively? What habits do you need to develop? Where should you focus your effort and attention? How do you find the courage to let go of your technical competence and become a professional leader? How do you motivate people to give more of themselves than even they thought possible?*

To answer these questions, you'll need to challenge yourself and your fundamental beliefs about what leadership is. If you've been around long enough to know that leadership is not as easy as it looks, you stand to gain an incredible amount from confronting yourself in this way. Keep reading.

The hurdle for more experienced executives to clear, though, is to answer a deeper question: *Has my success to date been attributable more to my intellect, experience, and business acumen than to my leadership capability and performance?* If so, keep reading.

No matter where each of us is in our leadership journey, we'd do well to take the advice of John Wooden, the iconic former UCLA basketball coach, who said, "It's what you learn *after* you know it all that counts."

LEADERSHIP CAPABILITY VS. BUSI-NESS ACUMEN

NO BULLSH!T LEADERSHIP doesn't replace formal business education and theoretical learning. What it does do is immediately put the practical tools and techniques for leading more effectively into the hands of every leader, from the *starry-eyed* novice to the jaded executive.

Being successful in the world of work still requires a good grounding in the foundational skills of business: finance, marketing, strategy, law, sales, operations, etc. But this isn't the secret to great leadership.

I'm reminded of an experienced manager, Eric, who was hired into a critical leadership position in one of my company's operational sites.

The first encounter I had with Eric was intriguing. We were at a social function immediately following a leadership workshop. The general manager to whom he reported introduced him to me as I chatted with our company's chairman. My immediate impression? Mad professor!

He was clearly very bright, and he had experience in asset-intensive industries, as the litany of previous senior positions on his résumé attested. But he was unable to engage with us in any meaningful way, even in a fairly relaxed and superficial conversation about his first few months with the company. It was more than just nerves—for me, this failure to connect was a red flag.

I later asked Eric's general manager how his new hire was settling in. He spoke to me in glowing terms about Eric's experience and track record, and also mentioned that he was MBA-qualified.

Despite this seemingly unassailable résumé, within six months or so, rumblings of his poor leadership performance started to reach my office. But when we held our biannual talent management and development sessions, the general manager would staunchly defend Eric, again referencing his experience, intellect, and education.

Unfortunately, the story on the ground was somewhat different. As CEO, I was accustomed to looking through the sometimes unforgiving lens of results—and the results from Eric's team remained *sub-standard*. What's more, his relationships with people in the head office, people whose help he needed to achieve his outcomes, were dysfunctional and fractured.

Whenever I visited that particular site, the people on his team would reluctantly confess that Eric communicated poorly and couldn't connect with them on an **inter-personal** level. His style was autocratic and directive. Still, the leaders between him and me weren't prepared to face those facts.

Here was a man with many years of experience, deep industry knowledge, and a *first-rate* business education who couldn't succeed in a senior role because he lacked the basic capability to *lead*. Being intelligent, experienced, and likable simply wasn't enough. There was no world in which Eric could build the platform of trust and commitment necessary to improve his team's performance.

So, after some not-so-subtle pressure from me, the inevitable parting of ways occurred.

Working with Eric, who was very capable by many measures, was just one of many experiences that proved to me that business acumen doesn't guarantee performance.

A good, strong business education is likely to include an MBA at some point, and I found the learnings from my MBA invaluable. I would even go so far as to say that if it weren't for my MBA, it's highly unlikely that I could have achieved what I did: a successful transition from IT project manager to general manager, moving seamlessly between job families, and eventually becoming CEO of a significant business.

But make no mistake: your MBA is the icing on the cake, not the cake itself. Your *experience* is the cake. What you learn in postgraduate business studies won't make you a better leader. In fact, I've seen some leaders' performance *decline* after completing their MBA, because not only did they fail to learn anything about leadership, they also acquired an extra dose of arrogance, making great leadership even more elusive for them. They started to believe their own bullshit.

Your ability to lead, get results, and drive performance is the cake. Your business education is the icing. And remember, no one over the age of 12 eats a bowl of icing on its own.

So, yes, business skills and knowledge are essential parts of a successful leader's repertoire. But this is necessary, not sufficient.

HOW TO GET THE MOST FROM THIS BOOK

NO BULLSH!T LEADERSHIP unveils a comprehensive leadership framework that's guaranteed to uplift the performance, capability, and confidence of even the most battle-hardened leader. In a world where knowledge has become a commodity like any other, this book cuts through the noise, delivering real-world insights that you won't find anywhere else. It's your road map for leadership success.

The principles described in this book aren't esoteric. They are deceptively simple but, if applied assiduously, incredibly powerful. They break down the complex permutations of human and organizational performance into their simplest form, giving you the opportunity to understand and apply the techniques to your individual context, regardless of the level you're currently operating at.

We start by exploring the problem with leadership: *Why are great leaders in such short supply? What makes a great leader? Should we be surprised that very few people in leadership positions ever accept the challenge of becoming leaders who are worthy of being followed by others?*

Chances are, like me, at some point in your career you've worked for a leader who couldn't manage a pig to get dirty. That's the last thing you'd want to become, right?

To address this, the core chapters provide a codified leadership system, which forms the bedrock upon which to build the culture of your team. If there's one thing I've learned in the course of my career, it's this: *Leadership drives culture; culture drives performance.*

There are seven fundamental principles in this leadership system, and I dedicate a chapter to each. These are imperative statements, because imperatives imply action. Imperatives are a call to arms for your commitment and focus. All too often we hear leaders say, "Yes, I know that!" Well, if you know, then why aren't you doing anything about it?

Knowing the principles of leadership no more builds your leadership capability than buying a gym membership gives you the perfect six-pack!

It's only through taking action on these seven leadership imperatives that you'll become a better leader.

Figure 1: The No Bullsh!t Leadership Framework

| Deliver Value

We start here, because this is core to everything a leader does. Your purpose is to deliver value for the stakeholders of your organization: customers, owners, employees, regulators, bankers, the communities in which you operate, etc. That's it. Period. It's all about value.

As a leader, your job is to work out what represents value in *your* context. Understanding what truly represents value is core to everything else you do. For example, if I'm given a choice between investing my company's resources into a project that yields additional profits, or one that keeps my people safer when they come to work, which should I choose?

A leader's job is to answer difficult and complex questions like this, and provide clarity for their people about what they need to do individually and collectively to create value. Without a laser-like focus on value, most of your people will just end up cranking the handle.

| Handle Conflict

The inability to handle conflict is the number one career killer for a leader. Almost everything we do when we take on the mantle of leadership involves some form of conflict. Unless we can handle conflict, we can't build a high-performing team. We can't negotiate successfully. We can't engage our best people in the decision-making process. Performance declines.

Conflict aversion is most often driven by a deep-seated need for acceptance—the need to be liked. And although it may be counterintuitive, a leader has to learn to overcome this instinct if they're to be truly successful. *Respect before popularity* is the mantra of the no bullshit leader.

| Build Resilience

Most senior leaders have developed a level of resilience that enables them to withstand the trials and tribulations of life in a large organization. Resilience is a critical piece in your repertoire.

Setbacks happen to everyone, but your success depends very much on how well you can manage these inevitable setbacks. Given many people's underdeveloped capacity for self-awareness, it's sometimes difficult to identify a lack of resilience in yourself.

How do you narrow the scope of a problem to make it more manageable? How do you develop the perspective to deal calmly with a crisis? And how do you eventually acquire the elusive state of *grace under pressure*?

| Work at the Right Level

It's so much easier when one of your team isn't doing their job properly to just step in and do it for them. Why? Because you can…because it makes you feel good…because it's easy to rationalize, "I always get the job done."

The problem is, you're *not* paid to do your people's jobs, you're paid to do your own. Understanding the difference between leading your people and doing their jobs for them will help you to avoid an ever-increasing workload. You can't ascend through the layers of an organization while still being indispensable to the functioning of your team.

Although it might seem a little perverse, your goal should be to make yourself redundant, *not* indispensable. If your team can't function without you, and the capability below you is weak, you make it difficult for your bosses to move you somewhere else. You start to look like someone who belongs in your current role, not the next level up.

| Master Ambiguity

For this generation of leaders, there's never been a more ambiguous time. The global COVID-19 pandemic has truly shaken the world order, broken the paradigms that we had taken for granted, and introduced a completely different set of strategic considerations, which no one had envisaged before this decade began.

The role of a leader, though, remains the same. As you take on accountability for more senior roles, a critical leadership capability is to sit comfortably in ambiguity, absorb the complexity and uncertainty of your environment, and then translate that uncertainty into tangible, concrete action for those you lead.

A leader doesn't have the luxury of succumbing to the temptation of lying in the fetal position until the ambiguity is resolved; the best of us even find a way to use ambiguity to steal a strategic march on our competitors.

| Make Great Decisions

Making better decisions faster than your competitors is a key determinant of your organization's ongoing success. Setting up a culture that values speed in decision-making, without allowing it to degenerate into a series of knee-jerk reactions, is a difficult balance for any leader to tread.

How do you know what makes a great decision? How do you muster the discipline to push yourself to act quickly and decisively amidst complexity and uncertainty? How do you unlock the knowledge and capability of the people around you? How do you acquire the right information? And how much information is enough?

I don't know any great leaders who aren't also great decision makers.

| Drive Accountability

One head to pat, one arse to kick. Simple.

Shared accountability is no accountability. But accountability and empowerment are symbiotic. How do you create an environment where people are truly empowered to make decisions and live with the consequences? Ultimately, people actually crave greater accountability, so letting them make their own decisions frees them up to pursue excellence.

Setting up clear accountabilities can be tricky, especially in today's organizations of ever-increasing structural complexity. But there are ways to implement a single-point accountability model even in complex, diverse, and matrix-driven organizations.

Lots of organizations have good strategies, but it's the ones who execute best that thrive, and this comes down to building a strong accountability culture.

To bring this all together, we have to be able to align these critical competencies and integrate the learnings into our existing leadership style. And everyone's style is different. We each have a unique leadership *fingerprint* that no one else can emulate.

The final chapter links all the concepts, tools, and practical techniques together in a way that will enable you to take the most relevant lessons for you, right now, and incorporate them into your toolkit. Although there might be 50 things you'd like to work on, having the discipline and focus to go after only the one or two changes that will make the most difference is the path to victory.

As you launch into this journey of discovery, remember that it's up to you to bring the words in this book to life. After all, it's not what you *know* that counts. It's not what you *believe* that counts. It's not what you *understand* that counts. And it's certainly not what you *say* that counts.

When you're a leader, it is what you *do* that counts.

CHAPTER 1

THE PROBLEM
WITH LEADERSHIP

THE BULLSH!T WE BELIEVE

Have you ever heard a leader say, "Our people are our greatest asset"? Maybe you've said it yourself. Some part of you may have even believed it.

I'm a huge fan of irony, and in these few words the irony is rich. The very comparison of people to other corporate assets—physical, financial, technical, etc.—dehumanizes them. It demonstrates precisely the lack of regard for individuals that this platitude is intended to alleviate.

If people were indeed the greatest asset of an organization, leaders would treat them very differently. In the vast majority of organizations, people are not the greatest asset, but rather the most *underutilized* asset.

If you value your assets, you treat them with the respect they deserve. You know how to get the most out of them. You don't run them into the ground—you maintain them well to preserve their useful life. You figure out how to leverage them to gain competitive advantage. You understand the value that they're capable of creating and spend deliberate effort thinking about how to capture that value.

If we're going to compare our people to other organizational assets, then we at least need to treat them with the same level of importance, don't we?

Imagine this scenario. You report to me as your direct manager, and you're conducting a negotiation on behalf of the organization. One day, you walk into my office and say, without the faintest hint of embarrassment, "Martin, you know that deal I'm negotiating? Well, we've done a thorough analysis of the risk and value drivers and understand our counterpart's position. We're confident that the value of the transaction is $100 million. But I was thinking last night... It's going to be really difficult to convince the other party of our position, and it'll take a lot of time and effort to get the deal done. Why don't we just settle now for $75 million and move on?"

That would be virtually unthinkable. To suggest leaving $25 million on the table, just because it looked as though capturing that value might be hard? As your boss, I'd be so shocked that I might even consider freeing you up to be successful in another organization (preferably, one of our competitors).

But often, when it comes to our people, leaving value on the table is exactly what we do. I've had senior executives say to me, with a straight face, "Martin, you know that vice president who's running our Atlantic region? Well, he isn't making the progress I expected. The culture of his team is very poor, and the results in his region aren't improving. I know you've been pushing me to do something about this. But I was thinking last night... The last time we filled that role, we found it really difficult to find the right person. At least the current VP has the right industry experience. Performance management would be difficult and time consuming, and I'm not sure it will change anything. Besides, I've got truckloads of other important things I need to focus on, so I'm not going to take any action at the moment."

For some strange reason, this doesn't sound quite as ridiculous as the first example. What would be unthinkable behavior in terms of financial outcomes (where results are tangible and quantitative) often appears acceptable when it comes to people, leadership, and culture (where measuring outcomes is more difficult).

And to compound the felony, in the next breath that same executive will tell me that his own leadership performance is excellent.

Until we stop believing our own bullshit about leadership, culture, and people, we'll never achieve the results we should. //

WHY IS LEADERSHIP HARD?

I don't know exactly when it happened, but the leadership discourse has devolved into a fluffy, abstract discussion on the aspirational qualities that great leaders should possess. *Great leaders are humble; great leaders are transparent; great leaders have integrity; great leaders lead from the front.*

Every year, millions of books, articles, blogs, and podcasts tell us how to be better leaders. We feel a warm glow of satisfaction when we consume this information, comforted by the impression that we're on the road to leadership excellence. Unfortunately, for the most part this guidance serves only to motivate us with a short-term sugar hit of inspiration. The advice isn't practical or specific enough to be of any real use.

It reminds me of an old Monty Python comedy sketch, a fictitious children's show called *How To Do It*, in which they parody our tendency to oversimplify very complex subjects. Amongst other topics, they tackle how to split the atom, how to construct box girder bridges and, my favorite, how to play the flute. Their explanation? "Well, kids, you blow in one end and move your fingers up and down the outside."

Absolutely true, but not particularly useful.

Most leadership advice is like that: true, but not useful.

Amidst the vast array of definitions of leadership, sometimes it's easier to describe what leadership *isn't*. It isn't about making people happy. It isn't about virtue signaling. It isn't about making sure that everyone gets along. It isn't about wielding the power of your position, either. It isn't about mindlessly doing whatever your bosses instruct you to do, nor is it about pandering to their whims. It isn't about accepting everyone unconditionally, regardless of their individual choices about how they behave and perform.

I've seen so many leaders over the course of my career pin their leadership credentials on one of these common fallacies. Virtue signaling is a particularly common weapon in many CEOs' arsenals. They're desperate to be seen as noble, benevolent leaders who have the interests of their people, and the greater good of society, as the dominant consideration driving every decision. This is some A-grade bullshit.

As you get to know them, you often find a jarringly different reality. The misalignment between how they wish to be perceived, what they truly believe, and how they ultimately act is sometimes difficult to fathom. Despite the facade of good intent, their behavior is driven almost entirely by their desire for personal rewards.

But if leadership isn't about these things, what *is* it about? Well, first and foremost, leadership is about results. My biggest bugbear with today's popular view on leadership is that it has decoupled the process of leading people from the essential need to achieve results. We seem to have lost sight of the fundamental purpose of leadership: value creation. And I don't simply mean financial value.

NO BULLSH!T LEADERSHIP re-establishes the connection between people and outcomes, with a simple, prime leadership objective: to deliver optimal results by getting the most from your people.

But to lead like this is hard. It sometimes pulls us in the opposite direction of our most primordial drives. It demands that we look at ourselves with a raw honesty that most prefer to shy away from. It parachutes us into situations that we'd rather avoid. It does nothing to build the illusion of self-assurance and confidence that we spend a lifetime trying to fabricate.

Leadership is hard because, more than anything else, it's about people. Most of us struggle to manage ourselves: our subconscious drivers, our relationships, our emotions, our mental health, our habits. Leadership demands not only that we master ourselves, but also that we become strong enough and capable enough to help others do the same.

People are complex and unpredictable, each individual a unique package informed by their childhood trauma, significant relationships, and the many choices that have brought them to where they are today. As leaders, we aren't necessarily equipped to deal with the myriad personalities, motivations, and expectations of our people. Besides, trying to cater to them would be futile, as the permutations are virtually limitless.

Taking on the mantle of leadership for the first time is a huge challenge. We effectively have to take a backward step. On Friday, I was an expert in my field, with deep skills in law, finance, or marketing. But now it's Monday, and I'm a leader—a complete novice. My role has changed from being responsible only for my own results, to taking accountability for the work of others. People who, incidentally, are unlikely to be as capable as me (after all, I was the one who got the promotion, not them!).

It's the lack of control we experience in this progression to a new type of role that's foreign and difficult, that pushes us to work below our level. To micromanage, to rescue, to over-function for our people. All so that we can remain comfortable in the knowledge that we're still valuable to the organization, and continue to deliver results through our own individual brilliance.

One of the great paradoxes of leadership is that the higher up you go, the less control you have over what happens day-to-day. There's also an inverse relationship to accountability—as you move into more senior roles, your accountability increases as rapidly as your direct control decreases. This, alone, is hard for many leaders to get their heads around.

How much control do you think Tony Hayward had, as chief executive of British Petroleum, over the decisions that were made many levels below him that led to the *Deepwater Horizon* oil spill in the Gulf of Mexico in 2010? Little control, full accountability—and he paid the price for that. But when you're a leader, that just comes with the territory.

Many aspects of leadership demand that we get comfortable with discomfort—for example, by walking into conflict situations willingly.

Human nature tells us that it's important that other people like us. In the earliest days of human evolution, remaining part of the tribe was a matter of life or death—this primal drive is at the very core of our survival instinct. Is it any wonder, then, that we shy away from situations of potential conflict that may result in us incurring the displeasure of our fellow humans?

However, if we don't willingly confront these situations, we'll never master the skills required to handle them. If you were trying to improve your golf game, your tennis forehand, or your skiing technique, avoiding the practice would be a great way to guarantee you wouldn't improve.

I remember when I first learned to ski in deep powder snow. I was brought up in Australia, where, in most years, what we call skiing would only pass for downhill ice skating in North America. Although the technique for skiing in powder snow is similar to the technique for skiing on hard-packed terrain, it feels completely different.

So when I found myself in Aspen, Colorado, in perfect, dry, thigh-deep powder snow, I was lost. I spent most of that first morning digging snow out of orifices I'd forgotten I had!

Here's what's interesting. I could have given up and said, "This is too hard. I'll find some nice groomed trails and just ski those." It would have been a legitimate response, and I would have enjoyed myself all the same. But guess what? The next time I found myself in deep powder snow, I would be just as lost and just as frustrated as I was on that first morning.

So I threw myself into it. How long did it take to become competent? I have no idea, but what I do remember is that at some point, it just started to work. It started to feel good. I had my balance, and I was floating through that powder as if I were starring in a Warren Miller movie. Sometimes you just need to put enough miles under the skis that it starts to feel OK.

Leadership is like this. When I first started leading people, I was as bad as anyone, and worse than most.

But when I came out of my first difficult conversation, something weird happened. I had the blinding realization that my ability to do this was a fundamental building block of competent leadership. Fortunately for me, I'm a little dysfunctional. So, just like I did in Aspen, instead of shying away from these difficult one-on-one situations, I threw myself into them.

I still recall, with great embarrassment, one of my early conversations with a team member who needed some performance feedback. I was impatient, disconnected, and arrogant. Without seeking to understand anything of the individual before me, I described why his performance was sub-standard, and what I thought needed to change for it to be considered acceptable. My solution? "If you can't do it, get out of the way and I will."

Despite my obvious ineptitude as a leader, I had just enough self-awareness to realize that this approach wasn't getting me or the team where we needed to be. So I decided to improve.

I drove myself to have as many difficult conversations as I possibly could. Learning, becoming more comfortable, still being terrible. Within a few years, I was more at ease having difficult conversations in a less confrontational way. I was even starting to understand the value of listening, rather than just imparting my own view of the situation.

I challenged people to stretch themselves, I coached them every step of the way, and then I confronted them when they needed my help to understand the consequences of the choices they were making. Over the years, I became the catalyst for a lot of people to make decisions about what type of job they *really* wanted, and many found their ideal, less demanding role elsewhere.

For others, I know that I was instrumental in their choice to improve their leadership capability and confidence.

One day, I woke up and realized that I had no fear of these situations. In fact, I actually looked forward to the opportunity to help someone improve their performance with the gift of targeted, specific, personally connected feedback. I also became really good at it—understanding what was driving people, reading their emotional state, seeing what made sense to them, and homing in on the things they didn't understand. My emotional intelligence grew rapidly.

Learning to become completely at ease in a potentially high-conflict environment is the best thing I ever did, and it's probably the most valuable skill I possess.

There are a number of these fundamental building blocks that leaders need to have in their toolkits in order to be capable, competent, and confident—to be able to provide the leadership that organizations need and people deserve. Competent leadership is a right, not a privilege, so if leadership is the path you choose, the fact that it's hard is irrelevant.

WHY ARE SO MANY LEADERS INEFFECTIVE?

Imagine if we put the same amount of time, energy, focus, and commitment into leadership as we did into our original career choice. For professionals, we spend years studying to become a doctor, an architect, a marine biologist. For tradespeople, we spend years becoming certified and gaining the competencies we need to do our jobs safely and effectively.

Yet when we're first thrust into a leadership position, we're given little guidance, limited training, and poor role models to learn from. Apparently, we're supposed to intuitively know what to do, or to learn complex and critical skills by osmosis.

In the absence of clear direction, we fall back on what we know best and what worked for us in the past. For many of us, it's completely counterintuitive that we originally chose our career based upon a preference for technical and task-focused work, yet we're now expected to become accomplished leaders, with an aptitude and drive to shape the performance and behavior of others. But this is often the only way we can progress to levels of greater status, authority, and remuneration, what society has told us are the measures of success.

You can skate by for quite a while on your intellect and cognitive ability as a proxy for leadership. But the higher up you go, the less individual impact you're able to have, and the more you'll need to rely on other people, some of whom are well removed from you in the hierarchy.

I've seen some leaders who thrive, and countless others who struggle with this transition.

The leaders who thrive appear to come to terms fairly early with the fact that they can't control every little detail, and they find other ways to achieve results. They channel their energy into enabling their people, by developing leadership bench strength and a high-performance culture. Rather than feeling increasingly insecure about the things they can't directly control, they're confident in the knowledge that their people can competently do the jobs they're paid to do.

The leaders who struggle never seem to overcome the dissonance of having to take greater accountability for outcomes they have less control over. These are the leaders who are prone to say to their closest friends and family, "Business would be a lot easier without the people."

The fear of letting go of our identity, coupled with the lack of recognition that leadership has intrinsic worth, holds us back from becoming great leaders. Our ineffectiveness is reinforced by the lack of effective leadership development. When we sense that we aren't particularly good at something, and we aren't given the guidance we need to improve, we naturally retreat to the things we *are* good at.

As we ascend to higher levels of leadership, there's an ever-greater need for us to learn but, paradoxically, more pressure not to admit that we don't know something. The dissonance that this creates can be overwhelming, and it's felt most by the people we lead.

That's what's so attractive about the superficial fluff of most leadership advice: we feel better about ourselves when we aspire to noble leadership virtues, which require no action from us whatsoever.

UNLOCKING DISCRETIONARY EFFORT

The quest to unlock your people's discretionary effort can be elusive, but it is arguably one of the most important leadership outcomes. This is central to NO BULLSH!T LEADERSHIP, so it's important to understand a little about what actually drives discretionary effort.

No one's going to get excited by the prospect of making more money for the shareholders. Many organizations deal with this by setting up bonus structures to align the interests of the owners and management of a business, shrewdly leveraging self-interest. Pay them to perform, and watch the money roll in, right?

There are two obvious problems with this approach.

First and foremost, putting incentives in place for the achievement of narrow financial objectives can have devastating side effects. Leaders often adopt myopic behaviors to guarantee their personal rewards, regardless of the trail of destruction left in their wake.

Examples of this abound in some of the more spectacular corporate lapses of recent memory: Halliburton's overcharging on government contracts; Volkswagen's emissions violations and fraudulent reporting; Wells Fargo's opening of bogus customer accounts to hit cross-selling targets; Enron's beyond-creative accounting to hide monumental financial losses. The thousands of documented cases like these are only the tip of the iceberg.

The second problem, according to the MIT Incentive Study,[1] is that monetary reward improves performance only for the most routine mechanical activities. When it comes to the higher cognitive processes, presumably the bread and butter of senior leadership roles, performance actually declines as the rewards increase.

Daniel Pink interpreted these results in his book *Drive: The Surprising Truth about What Motivates Us*. Pink's conclusion (spoiler alert) was that human motivation is driven by three things: autonomy, mastery, and purpose.

Autonomy and mastery are clearly evident in the **NO BULLSH!T LEADERSHIP** framework. But communicating a genuine, unambiguous purpose to rally your people around can be challenging. That's why senior leaders (often fresh from pocketing their personal bonuses) need to focus on this. Why should your people bother to give their best? What's in it for them? If you asked them to work to a higher standard, why would they (other than the fear of losing their jobs)?

Your people will be much better disposed to offer their discretionary effort if they understand a higher purpose and their role in achieving it. Communicating the purpose relentlessly, and helping people to find individual meaning, is an essential leadership endeavor.

The greatest opportunity to motivate comes when leaders manage to align their people to the core objectives of the organization, from top to bottom, with no loss of connection in between. It starts at the top with purpose, flows through organizational strategy, into tactical and operational plans, and eventually lands with extreme clarity at the frontline level.

---

1 Ariely, Dan, Uri Gneezy, George Loewenstein, and Nina Mazar. "Large Stakes and Big Mistakes." *Review of Economic Studies* 76, no. 2 (2009): 451–69. https://doi.org/10.1111/j.1467-937x.2009.00534.x.

How do I fit into this picture, and what do I need to do today to contribute to the organization's success?

I call this the school photo principle: people aren't capable of looking at the bigger picture until they can see where they fit.

WHAT BARRIERS DO LEADERS FACE?

Leadership takes commitment and discipline. It requires a dedicated approach to self-mastery, which starts with self-awareness. It requires the formation of good habits that are difficult to embed, particularly when they run counter to our psychological and emotional drivers.

We all have subconscious barriers that hold us back. We view the world through a lens that incorporates all of our intellect, wisdom, and experience. But it also incorporates all of our biases, fears, and unmet expectations.

I'm often reminded of Chris, an executive who worked for me several years ago, who had all the makings of a great leader. He was very intelligent, and he cared about his people. He was a good decision maker and understood the role of accountability and empowerment in delivering superior results. His people liked working for him, he was well respected, and he looked to be on the fast track to bigger and better career roles.

Unfortunately, I eventually formed the opinion that Chris had a fatal flaw. Whenever his views were challenged by his peers, particularly in a group setting, he became withdrawn, defensive, and negative. In that moment, he would cease to function in any useful way. Chris's involuntary response rendered him completely unable to engage calmly and logically in robust debate.

This behavior was debilitating for the leadership team. I believe strongly in the value of constructive tension between team members as a means of discovering the highest-quality outcomes. But the tension generated by Chris's behavior was laced with resentment and animosity, and it created an unnecessarily negative climate in the leadership team.

What's worse, Chris didn't leave his resentment in the boardroom. His frustration spilled over to his own people. This eventually manifested in a number of unhealthy cultural markers: Chris's team began to feel unappreciated and undervalued. What's worse, they started to develop a siege mentality. They saw themselves as the good guys, fighting against enormous odds and frequent interference to get the best result for the organization. Apparently, the rest of us weren't.

The culture that Chris was unwittingly creating could have easily developed into a case of Nut Island Effect. This is a phenomenon observed at the Nut Island sewage treatment plant in Boston, the subject of a 2001 *Harvard Business Review* article that exposed the root causes of the catastrophic failure of the facility before it was decommissioned in 1997.

The good people working at the Nut Island plant felt a deep distrust for management, became increasingly isolated, and began to write their own rules. As they were achieving strong results, the temptation for management to look the other way was compelling, but eventually this led to a stalemate that could only ever have been broken by the imminent crisis.

Fortunately, unlike the management of Boston's Metropolitan District Commission at that time, I've never been one to look the other way. I strengthened the governance mechanisms that were in place to oversee the performance of Chris's team and actively encouraged additional scrutiny on the decisions they made.

I also worked closely with Chris to ensure that he understood how his behavior was playing out and what impacts it had on those around him. I hired a top-notch executive coach to work with him, and I personally invested an incredible amount of time and energy into his executive development. But despite all of this, Chris couldn't manage to overcome this weakness.

This is just one example of how difficult it can be to become a great leader, even when you have the vast majority of attributes that would generally make you successful. In Chris's case, his lack of resilience is so deep-seated that despite all of the support he was given, it's unlikely he'll ever overcome it. It's anchored in emotional triggers that even he doesn't understand very well.

This doesn't necessarily mean that Chris can't be effective, perform well, and add value to the organizations he works for during his career. What it does mean, though, is that he'll always be held back from being his best until he overcomes this problem.

Leadership requires a delicate balance to provide the opportunity and environment for someone to consistently perform at their peak without usurping their personal accountability for making that happen. This requires a level of emotional intelligence that most of us don't innately possess.

It's also complicated by the fact that we're not, for the most part, held to account for doing the core work of leadership. If my boss doesn't model the discipline and practice of competent leadership, then I know she isn't going to be up my ribs for not doing the difficult work of leadership myself.

People generally follow their boss's lead when trying to work out what's expected. If you don't diligently manage performance standards, then there's no chance that the leaders below you will either. In fact, even when you *do* manage performance standards diligently, some of your leaders *still* won't do it. In general, the behaviors, standards, and expectations that you set will be increasingly diluted at each level below you.

In the absence of a compelling road map for improving your leadership performance in a way that empowers you to deliver results, you might search high and low for that special potion that enables you to magically improve and to be confident and capable in a leadership role.

But there are no magical potions. We'd all like to have model-like good looks, great relationships, a stellar career, and $10 million in the bank. But that doesn't mean we're willing to do the work, to make the sacrifices, to accept the risk, or to demonstrate the perseverance that would actually make these outcomes a reality. So we continue to dream and wish it were different…and stay exactly where we are.

The most insurmountable barriers that we face are contained within the six inches between our ears. It's only by having the willingness to change our fundamental beliefs, to put someone else's interests before our own, and to do things that seem unnatural, that we improve as leaders.

CUTTING THROUGH THE BULLSH!T

In order to cut through and *really* change the way you lead, it's important to reflect on where you are now. Of all the desirable leadership attributes, self-awareness is arguably the most important. Why? Because self-awareness and reflection are prerequisites to understanding what you need to change.

For senior leaders, the ability to reflect is often the only thing that stands between humility and hubris. Many leaders won't open this book, because it's so much easier to believe their own bullshit.

At the end of each chapter, I give you the opportunity to answer a few simple questions and rate where you currently stand. This will help you to reflect and make some concrete decisions about what you intend to implement from that chapter.

SO, WHERE ARE YOU NOW?

There are a number of fundamental problems we encounter with leadership. We often focus on the wrong things. We avoid situations that might cause conflict. We bury ourselves in busywork. We find it difficult to relinquish control.

For each of the following questions, rate yourself (on a scale of 1 to 10) before you move on to the next chapter. This will give you greater insight into what stands between you and leadership excellence.

1. How comfortable are you when conflict situations arise?

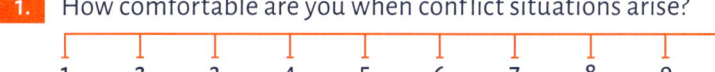

2. How difficult do you find it to let go of control when someone on your team is undertaking an important task?

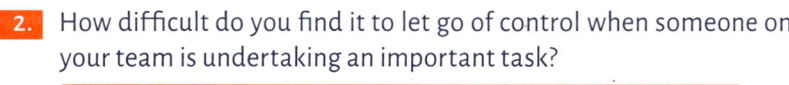

3. How reliant are you on your capability, intellect, and experience in order to do your job?

4. How do you rate your ability to connect and engage with people?

5. To what extent is your identity still tied up in your technical discipline?

6. To what extent do you wield the power of your position to get results?

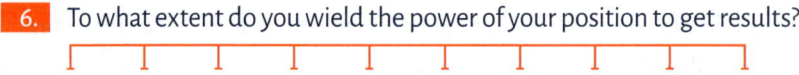

7. How much of your focus each week do you place on developing your people?

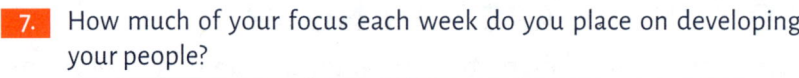

8. Do you have good leadership role models around you to learn from?

9. Based upon what you've learned in this chapter, how strong a leader do you think you are?

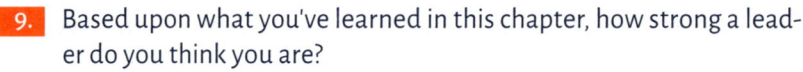

CHAPTER 2

DELIVER
VALUE

THE BULLSH!T WE BELIEVE

As leaders, we're continually encouraged to focus on developing aspirational personal attributes: transparency, humility, fallibility, integrity, consistency, etc.... If you embody these attributes, you're sure to become a great leader, right? Some pundits even suggest that you should *fake it until you make it.*

This is complete bullshit. Even though developing any of these positive attributes might ultimately make you a better person, it won't necessarily make you a better leader. Why? Because focusing solely on aspirational attributes misses the whole point of leadership.

As a leader, you're not there simply to be a personal role model. You're there to create value.

Being transparent can be crucial in building trust, but it won't help you one iota if you don't possess the interpersonal skills to convey ideas and seek alignment from your team.

Being fallible can be an accelerator for creating the right culture, but if that fallibility is coupled with incompetence, it'll have the opposite effect: your people will lose confidence in you.

Being humble is an essential counterbalance to hubris, but if that humility is coupled with timidity, you won't be able to get results. It'll just mean that you're less likely to set high standards of performance, effectively dooming your team to mediocrity.

No, leadership isn't about your aspirational personal attributes—it's about creating value. Period. And before you rail indignantly against the seemingly mercenary nature of this concept, it's important to recognize that value can come from many different sources. It can come just as readily from enhanced community outcomes, reduced environmental impact, or safer operating conditions as it can from superior financial performance.

But no matter how you define it, you need to understand that the only reason your organization exists in the first place is to create value for its stakeholders. It's also the only reason an organization hires leaders. Until you acknowledge this fact at a visceral level, you'll always struggle to do the work of leadership. Why would you take on difficult or unpopular issues if you didn't genuinely believe in the ultimate value this would create?

Forget the aspirational attributes for now. Instead, as you wade deeper into these pages, focus on the incredible value that you can bring to your people by becoming a stronger leader. If you can accept that it's all about value creation, this opens the door to uncovering the highest-value outcomes for the context *you* operate in: your industry, your market, your organization, this point in time. //

WHAT IS VALUE?

Everything a leader does must be directed toward delivering the greatest value possible. That's why it's important to define value as clearly and simply as you can. Your people will respond much better to everything you do, every decision you make, and every initiative you embark upon if they can readily see how it creates value.

Value starts with the organization's purpose: Why do we exist, and for whom? It then flows down through strategy, tactical planning, and operational targets. The greater the alignment of objectives from top to bottom, the more likely you'll be able to lead your people to deliver real value.

The word *value* immediately brings to mind financial results, but value actually comes in a wide variety of forms. Let's look at a few examples of how different sources of value can deliver results—and discuss how complex the decisions about different types of value can become.

| Financial Value

This type of value gets the most attention. It's highly quantifiable and, more often than not, it's the measure that's most closely coupled with an organization's ability to survive and grow. Financial outcomes are also the primary means by which people are rewarded.

Delivering financial value seems obvious. It's easy to measure success or failure when you're looking at the bottom line. But evaluating which of several investments is most attractive is not as easy as it might sound.

For example, a CEO on the path of growth by acquisition will often overvalue a potential asset or takeover target. They want it, therefore it must be valuable. It's axiomatic that companies will pay over the odds for assets they really want to own.

An example of this hubris is global mining behemoth Rio Tinto's purchase of the Riversdale mine in Mozambique in 2011. At the height of the commodities boom, when prices and egos soared, and competition to snap up the best assets was intense, Rio paid $3.7 billion for the mine. Within two years of acquisition, the value of the mine was written down by $2.9 billion. Not long thereafter, in 2014, Rio sold the mine for a mere $50 million, recovering a little over 1 percent of the price they paid for it three years earlier. This was undoubtedly a key factor in the resignation of then–chief executive Tom Albanese.

A cursory look across listed company balance sheets reveals that Riversdale is by no means an isolated case. Overpayments for assets often turn up in the annual accounts as write-downs when the assets are impaired. And when companies overpay to acquire other businesses, the gap between what the business was truly worth and what the acquiring company paid for it sits on the balance sheet as an *intangible* asset.

If it's this hard to choose between the financial investments that will drive the greatest value for your business, you can imagine the difficulty in comparing and ranking these against potential investments that are based upon less quantitative value criteria.

| Customer-Driven Value

No organization can exist without customers. There are many ways to deliver value for your organization through the customer. Obvious examples involve delivering products and services that represent superior value over others that are available in the market. But customer value can also be created indirectly by, for example, investing in a better understanding of your customers' needs or building your brand to drive greater customer loyalty.

Some years ago, when I was a senior vice president responsible for sales and marketing at a large publicly listed transport company, we invested heavily in getting to know the customer better. When negotiating long-term, high-value contracts, often measured in the hundreds of millions of dollars, knowing how to better meet our customers' needs created a real competitive edge.

We developed a playbook for a few dozen of our major customers. We invested in market intelligence and research that enabled us to see the world through their eyes. We scrutinized and documented their business strategies, the levers they pulled to drive profits, their past performance, their risk profiles, their asset lives, and their market outlook. We even spent time debating the motives and interests of their key decision makers. You name it, we analyzed it!

This investment in customer intelligence enabled us to secure billions of dollars' worth of long-term contracts over a two-year period, at a strike rate of around 90 percent. Was that a value-driven investment of the organization's resources? With the benefit of hindsight, *absolutely*! But what if we'd only managed a 40 percent strike rate? Would that still have been money well spent? *Probably.* Could we have achieved the same result without spending as much on customer intelligence? *Possibly.* Even in a clear-cut example like this, there is a level of subjectivity and it requires astute judgment to make the right value-based decisions.

| Value from Improved Governance, Risk, and Compliance

The last several years have heralded a growing awareness and focus on governance, risk, and compliance (GRC). The value of improving GRC controls is difficult to quantify. You pretty much only notice them when they fail. But, as Warren Buffett famously said, "If a cop follows you for 500 miles, you're going to get a ticket."

We covered a few examples of corporate failure in the previous chapter. Failures seem to be most prevalent in the financial sector, where temptation and moral hazard have the strongest gravitational pull. Win-at-all-cost cultures and personal financial rewards can entice individuals to act in ways that they wouldn't under other circumstances. The necessity for investing in a robust GRC framework to manage this risk is obvious. But determining the *right* amount to invest is not.

You need to have protections in place to ensure your people paint within the lines but, equally importantly, you need to demonstrate to investors and regulators that GRC is actually a priority. How much is the right amount of money to invest, and how do you measure the value that comes from reducing the likelihood of brand damage?

| Value through Risk Reduction

Another form of value is risk reduction. Leaders have to understand the risks their organizations face. Managing risk is one of the primary obligations of a company's board of directors, but it's also a key responsibility for leaders at every level.

Knowing how much to invest in operational risk reduction can be vexed. Consider an operating power plant, which is designed to run 24-7 and only come offline for major maintenance every three or four years. Any interruption to operations in between these major overhauls can be very costly.

In a large, efficient power plant, an unplanned outage could cost an organization around $1 million per day in revenue. Knowing this, it's imperative to understand the risk of certain failure modes and to have contingency plans in place to get the plant up and running again quickly.

Reducing the risk of an extended plant outage creates enormous potential value for the organization. For example, many components of the plant are expensive to produce, and rarely needed, so you're not going to just find them sitting on a shelf at Home Depot. They need to be ordered from a specialist supplier, who might take three months to manufacture and deliver that critical part.

Even if the likelihood of failure is relatively low, the potential consequences are so great (losing $1 million of revenue every day for three months) that it may warrant holding a part like this in inventory to reduce the risk level of a failure. Conventional wisdom says (sensibly) that value comes when you reduce inventory to the lowest possible level. But holding a $300,000 part to potentially mitigate a $90 million loss, just in case something goes wrong, would appear to be a pretty smart decision.

Value through Safety Improvements

In any manufacturing business or heavy industry, your people's safety is critical. Anything a leader can do to reduce the likelihood of people getting hurt on the job is money well spent. But how far should you go? There will always be things that you could choose to spend more money on, but no business has a blank check. Deciding how to deliver high-value safety interventions while balancing the financial cost of doing so can tax the ingenuity of even the most capable leader.

I learned a very important lesson about this many years ago. I was touring a DuPont manufacturing facility in Parkersburg, West Virginia. The plant was commissioned in 1948 and had begun to show the natural wear and tear you'd expect from an asset of its vintage.

At that time, DuPont had a reputation for being the world's leading authority on industrial safety, and the purpose of the tour was to learn from that facility's management team about their approach to safety leadership.

As we walked around the 170-odd-acre plant, I noticed that the concrete walkways were in a state of disrepair—there were dozens of potential trip hazards. When I asked the plant manager why DuPont didn't fix it, he gave a pretty compelling answer.

To rip up and replace all of the pathways across the plant would have cost millions of dollars. Instead, they decided to visit the local hardware store, purchase a few cans of fluorescent-yellow spray paint, and spray over the top of the cracks, clearly marking them and aiding visibility.

Instead of spending millions of dollars to engineer the hazard out entirely, they spent a few hundred dollars on paint, plus a few hours of inspection and diligence from the leadership. "Now you can clearly see where the cracks are, so step over them!"

This was a great lesson for me in how to create value in one area (safety), while balancing the impact on another (financial). Perhaps the end result wasn't pretty, but it certainly was effective.

Value from Greater Efficiency and Productivity

We can always find more efficient and productive ways to do things. Leaders should strive to create a culture where people are constantly on the lookout for ways to do the job better, faster, or cheaper. How do we improve our work practices? Where are the bottlenecks in the process, and how do we overcome them? How do we streamline the procedure to make it *fit for purpose*? There is enormous value to be created here.

The Value of Business Continuity Planning

I suspect there were very few, if any, organizations on the

planet that had plans in place for the type of scenario we experienced with the COVID-19 pandemic. Overnight, offices were closed, transportation networks were shut down, and standard methods of communication and interaction had to be almost entirely reimagined.

Having now been through this experience, the need to build and test robust business continuity plans is more obvious. But, once again, you could invest an inordinate amount of time, energy, and money into preparing for every foreseeable eventuality. How would you choose between making an investment to reduce the risk of potential shocks to your business, industry, or country, or making an investment in a new product that will capture greater financial profits? What's the value calculus?

This list is by no means exhaustive. A leader's job is to assess the relative value of any investment to enable prudent decision-making across the broad spectrum of value sources. The common criterion is that every investment of an organization's resources must have a clear value outcome, whether it's reduced risk, greater profit, or better compliance.

Communicating this can be tricky. The ultimate aim is to give people absolute clarity about how the things they're asked to do on a day-to-day basis contribute to the highest-order objectives of the organization. Without a clear connection to purpose and value, your people will mostly end up just going through the motions.

All of these examples also demonstrate how difficult it can be to understand where the greatest value can be found, even within a common category. Once you start comparing the value of investing resources across *different* categories, the difficulty increases by an order of magnitude.

The most important thing is not necessarily to come up with definitive answers on any of these choices, but to engage in the discussions that lead to a better understanding of where the potential sources of value truly lie. As President Eisenhower once said, "Plans are worthless, but planning is everything."

ACTIVITY VS. VALUE

The only thing I know for certain about your organization is that you'll never have enough time, money, or people to do everything you'd like to do. That means you have to make deliberate choices about how and where to deploy your scarce resources to create the most value. As Michael E. Porter, widely considered to be the founder of the modern strategy field, once said, "The essence of strategy is choosing what *not* to do."

Simple, appropriate, high-value targets are an essential part of execution. Before you worry about efficiency and productivity, make sure you're working only on those things that really matter. Lose the weight first, then buy the new suit!

One of the most difficult things to do in any organization is to stop the activity that doesn't yield the highest value but is already in train. It's a lot easier to prevent something from ever starting than it is to stop something midstream.

The biggest challenge I faced as a CEO was not the complexity of our markets, the regulatory strictures, or the fluctuating reliability of our assets. It was the challenge of stopping the non-value-adding work that was being undertaken throughout the organization. It was like comfort food to our people, and it predictably created sclerosis in the organization's arteries.

The first step to overcome this is to clearly define what things drive the greatest value, and to direct your people toward accomplishing those outcomes in the most effective way. The second, and relatively more difficult step, is to eliminate everything else.

Discovering the Highest-Value Tasks

Working out what to do is all about choosing from the menu of proposed work, and making decisions about which of these to invest in. If you say it fast enough, it sounds easy.

But how do you actually decide which activities add the most value?

The first step is to develop the language of value with your people. They need to know that nothing should be done for its own sake, or simply because an individual is highly committed to the work. Everything has to be assessed on the basis of value before it can be initiated.

A really good way to develop the language of value is to think about the sales concept of features versus benefits. *Features* describe the properties of a product or service, whereas *benefits* describe the value that these features can create for you.

Let's look at the humble teaspoon. It has certain *features*—for example:

- It's approximately 6 inches long

- It's fabricated from stainless steel

- Its shape consists of a handle adjoining a concave bowl

- The bowl is oval-shaped, about an inch long, and half an inch wide

- The edge of the bowl may be slightly sharp for rudimentary cutting

Whilst all of this is interesting, it gives me absolutely no clue as to why I might want to use a teaspoon. However, once we focus on the *benefits* of the teaspoon, it becomes obvious almost immediately:

- The teaspoon is a perfect delivery system for 5 grams of sugar into a cup of coffee

- It can then be used to stir the coffee once the sugar has been introduced

- It's also the perfect implement for eating a boiled egg from its shell

Once you change your language from focusing on features to benefits, or activity to value, the whole conversation changes. This will increase the likelihood that you can build a work program that delivers the highest value for your organization.

Eliminating Low-Value Activity

There are several reasons why it's difficult to identify and eliminate low-value activity. Once something is started, it tends to take on a life of its own. The people undertaking the work will not only resist shutting it down, but often will actively try to conceal the fact that the work is being done.

Why do people have a tendency to want to continue their habitual activity, even when they intuitively sense that it isn't delivering value?

- We all like to do things that we enjoy, and that we can complete in a reasonably competent fashion, without having to stretch ourselves too far. Once we've built this type of work into our routine, we're reluctant to have it replaced. Any new work might not be as enjoyable—or we might not be as good at it.

- Many people find comfort in predictability. It's good to know what to expect when you head into the office each day, and a work program that shifts around too much can create an unwelcome level of uncertainty.

- One of the more dominant drivers is job security. If you're busy, then what you're doing must be important: How could they possibly do without you? Look at all the work you're doing. But if the work goes away, maybe your job goes away too.

- Many leaders hold onto low-value work to increase the scale of their portfolios: they're empire-building. This can push them to seek an ever-expanding scope and volume of activity for their teams, requiring a greater allocation of the organization's resources. This normally brings with it greater power (and remuneration).

With these implicit and explicit behavioral drivers in play, is it any wonder that it's so difficult to stop activity that should never have been started in the first place?

There are a few methods for attacking non-value-adding work so that it can be replaced with higher value alternatives. Here are a few suggestions:

| Work from a Zero Base

One of the most obvious ways to eliminate non-value-adding activity is to build your work program from a zero base. Most annual planning cycles are dominated by the continuation of existing work (and resource) commitments, and then introducing additional work.

Starting with a zero base demands that people challenge everything: justification is required not only to gain approval for commencing new activities, but to continue those that are already underway. The annual planning process is your first, best bet for pruning work that doesn't deliver value, so do everything you can at this point to construct the highest-value work program possible.

Stop Rewarding Inputs

We all tend to reward people for their hard work and, yes, there's a lot to be said for its virtue. But as long as we focus on this, we can't focus on value. What if one of your people works 12-hour days, and they're working on things that create almost no value?

If you focus on inputs, people will be rewarded regardless of what they've produced or delivered. Measuring value can only come from observing and rewarding outcomes. If someone can achieve high-value outcomes in four hours each day, that's better than someone creating less value in 12 hours.

Of course, if someone is cruising along on four-hour days, I'm sure you'll find something else for them to do. The point is, if it doesn't drive value, don't do it at all.

Rank the Work (Don't Prioritize It)

Most leaders and organizations like to prioritize, which is a useful way of describing the relative importance of any work item. Unfortunately, this can be really loose. Have you ever heard someone say, "I'm too busy to look at that; I'm already working on six priority ones." It prevents us from understanding the relative value of different items.

Simply assigning priority levels to action items doesn't enable the clarity and precision that's required to make prudent decisions as new work emerges. Not only does it become an excuse for not delivering something ("I'm too busy..."), but it enables poor behavior from above ("I don't care, just get it done...") when it isn't clear which pieces of work will deliver the greatest value.

That's why the discipline of ranking initiatives is so vital. It enables you to take a large work program and decide which is the most important initiative, the second-most important, the third-most, and so on. This leaves you with a clear (albeit flexible) ranking of priorities for everything your team does. It also makes any future conversations about the work program quite simple: *Will this new piece of work create more value for us than something on our existing list? If so, where would it fit against the current value rankings?*

SIMPLICITY AND FOCUS

In my five years as CEO of a large energy utility, we placed a huge focus on rebuilding the foundations of the business. This required a complete overhaul of the leadership capability through every layer of the company, and a 180-degree shift from being engineering-driven to value-driven. Execution was generally poor, requiring a complete change in cultural expectations, particularly around individual accountability.

I learned when I first took over the company that when it came to operational performance, simplicity and focus weren't on the menu. As if the convoluted planning processes and jargon-laden excuses weren't enough, there was a cavernous gap between the investment we made in our operating assets (the power stations) and their actual performance. I found this incredibly frustrating.

Eventually, after struggling with two operational executives (good people who couldn't shift the performance needle), I promoted a high-potential leader to the role of chief operating officer. From his first hour in the job, the new COO established his intent by delivering an important message to his people, particularly the general managers who ran the operating assets.

"Forget anything you've been doing up to now. This business is simple. We're going to focus on three things and three things only: safety, volume, and cost. If you're doing something that doesn't directly contribute to those three things, then stop. If we do the right things to focus on these three, the performance of our business will massively improve." And it did! The operations leaders in the field started to focus their people on the few things that made a real difference to performance.

They focused on increasing the percentage of time that tradespeople spent actually performing maintenance tasks, rather than just talking about them. This had the dual impact of improving the volume of output from the power stations (because more preventative maintenance was carried out), and reducing cost (because fewer contractors were required to carry out essential work that couldn't be handled by the core team).

They invested time and money into more efficient management of the coal stockpiles that fueled the plant. This was essential in removing bottlenecks that often caused the power stations to run at a reduced capacity, forgoing valuable returns.

And they learned to let go of the many nice-to-have projects that didn't result in a safer working environment. Instead of putting good money after bad by tweaking the written safety procedures, they focused on the practical things that really made the plant safer: better analysis and mitigation of the high-consequence/low-likelihood risks that could potentially cause a fatality.

Activity for its own sake often hides in complexity. Your people may unwittingly increase the complexity of any given task so that they can hold onto its mystique and the workload that, at least in their minds, reinforces their indispensability.

There are some good rules of thumb to ensure that, as a senior leader, you can shift the focus from attempting to get more and more things done, regardless of their relative value, to only going after the *right* things. Here are five practical ways to protect the culture of simplicity and focus:

1. Encourage leaders to free up their workloads.

A subtle shift is required here. All your conversations have to focus on the value that simplicity unlocks. Your language, target setting, and measurement of outcomes has to be expressed in these terms. Push your people to think about the things they're *eliminating*. Talk about how that frees up valuable resources to do other work, where their efforts deliver more value to the organization, and how the reduced workload and complexity improves their overall likelihood of success.

2. Push leaders to remove activities during the annual planning cycle.

We've covered the opportunity that exists in the annual planning cycle. For many organizations, once something ends up in an annual plan, it's a *fait accompli*, regardless of how the economics, value opportunity, or risks change over time. Using the annual planning cycle to rank, challenge, and kill the majority of the proposed work items will eliminate low-value activity before it gets a life of its own.

3. Create a culture where less is best.

Reward people for doing the right things, not for toiling endlessly on busywork. Never praise activity-weighted inputs like time in the office. Ignore these indicators. Reward and praise those who've reduced work and created higher-value outcomes for the organization.

4. **Don't enable your teams by throwing resources at a problem.**

People have a tendency to seek more resources, because resources are generally constrained. They'll always find a way to deploy these if you let them. Throwing money or people at a problem simply enables your team to perpetuate their bad habits. More resources does *not* equal greater value. More often than not, additional resources just increase complexity and diffuse your focus. This is the exact opposite of what we're trying to achieve.

5. **Expect your leaders to explain.**

It's important to listen for echoes: Are your leaders talking about their few key objectives? Are they constantly pushing to get greater clarity and focus people on what they need to do to really deliver value? It's one thing for the CEO to give an impassioned speech to the troops to talk about these principles, but if the leaders below aren't replicating the passion, drive, and commitment to simplifying the work program, they aren't doing their jobs.

If you can embed the drive for simplicity and focus into the culture of your team, you'll find the results are staggering. The challenge comes from the fact that the vast majority of people will resist this push. It takes an uncommon strength of leadership to chase simplicity with a relentless passion and drive that's sometimes difficult to find, even for the most committed among us.

EXCELLENCE OVER PERFECTION

As a young project manager, I ran a software development project for a large corporate client to analyze growth trends and congestion in urban traffic flows. It was quite a complex undertaking, and the client had some very knowledgeable and experienced people who provided the input requirements to the development team. I wanted to live up to their high standards.

My project team missed a deadline to deliver one of the components of the system to the client for acceptance testing. There had been delays perfecting the algorithm used to perform a particular calculation, and I wanted it to be perfect before we submitted it to the customer.

The client, Roger, called me into his office, sat me down, and just smiled as he said, "Martin, I know you want this calculation to be perfect, but we don't need it to be perfect." That was a surprise. "For a start, the analysis we do on this data is only for predicting trends, not coming up with precise answers. And secondly, this is why we have acceptance testing. We don't need you to deliver a perfect product, just one that's good enough for us to put through its paces so that we can find the bugs and fix them."

This was both revealing and liberating. We've all heard of the Pareto Principle: 80 percent of the results come from 20 percent of the effort. In other words, you can very quickly get to a point of excellence, but improving the outcome beyond that requires more and more time and energy.

Eventually, we reach the point of diminishing returns, where any additional effort expended on a task is unproductive. On the road to perfection, this point comes much sooner than you might imagine.

Over the years, I've seen engineers, lawyers, accountants, and marketers all striving for a level of perfection that's incredibly costly and counterproductive. It can slow an organization's tempo to glacial speed, with very little upside in return.

The pursuit of perfection is often seen as desirable, even noble. *We accept only the highest standards and do whatever it takes to meet them.*

When we hear that, it sounds inspiring. But it's also deeply flawed. The culture created by perfectionism is surprisingly destructive. No one wants to take responsibility for an outcome that might not be perfect (and nothing ever is). So they seek to avoid the accountability that comes with delivering their objectives.

Perfectionism is also surprisingly safe. As long as you're engaged in the worthwhile cause of perfecting something, it can't be completed, and therefore opened up for critique or rejection. Perfectionism softens our fear of failure by giving it a different label. Instead of saying, "I'm afraid this won't be good enough," we say, "I'm doing everything I can to make sure this is perfect."

But, ultimately, perfectionism reinforces the concept of activity for its own sake, losing sight of the value imperative. Perfectionist leaders send the signal that your best simply isn't good enough, as they keep sending you back to refine work to a point where any potential value is inevitably destroyed.

A culture of excellence over perfection, on the other hand, has some incredible benefits. It empowers people to take control of their work and make sensible judgments about the level of quality required in any given scenario. It encourages them to have a crack at something, without fear of the outcome being less than perfect.

When people are allowed to make mistakes, they learn and gain confidence, which in turn builds capability in the team. It liberates them to build momentum through a sensible balance of outcome quality and speed. To create a culture like this, you have to let people make some mistakes. It's often said, "Good judgment comes from experience, and experience comes from bad judgment."

Pursuit of excellence rather than perfection is much more likely to see you reach the highest standards. Excellence is about *momentum*: keep moving, keep improving, adapt as you go. Perfection is about *inertia*: don't do anything until it's 100 percent right.

Creating a culture of excellence over perfection requires you to adopt some simple principles and language to continually reinforce the behaviors you're looking for. Bear in mind, though, that this has to be more than slogans and catchphrases: if you're trying to shift a perfectionist culture, you'll need to pursue this with a high level of intensity. Here's a few suggestions for how to pull it off:

1. **Reward the pursuit of excellence, especially when it results in failure.**

Look for those instances where people demonstrate that they're moving forward fearlessly to achieve excellent outcomes, and reward them. One-on-one feedback is a great way to do this, but public recognition and praise is even better. Using the power of storytelling broadly throughout the organization consolidates the concept and reaffirms the behaviors you're seeking.

Although it's sometimes difficult to overlook spectacular failures, this is when it's even more important to reinforce the concept of excellence over perfection. When a project fails, go back to basics and ask yourself the questions:

- Did this person undertake their actions with the right intent?

- Did they follow the required governance processes?

- Did they exercise sound judgment and pursue rational actions?

- Did they act within their remit and accountability?

- Did their behavior align with the organization's values?

If you can answer yes to these questions, then the person shouldn't be crucified for their failure, but rewarded for having the courage to take a calculated risk. Obviously, though, if they continue to produce a litany of failures, you'll need to have a different conversation.

2. **Focus your people on the underlying risk.**

At its essence, decision-making is about risk. *How much risk am I prepared to take in order to attain the expected rewards?* Conversely, if something you decide to do fails, what risk do you expose the organization to?

Understanding the inherent risks associated with any decision will help to inform your view on how close to the Pareto 80 percent you need to be. Some things can happily be 70 percent accurate without any great bearing on the outcome, whereas others have to be as close to the 95 percent mark as you can get them. Nothing ever gets to 100 percent. (Nothing. Ever.)

For example, a weekly flash report that gives management an early view of financial performance can be pretty rough: it's just a ballpark. Seventy percent accuracy might be perfectly acceptable for a report like this but wouldn't be good enough for the monthly financial report to the board of directors. That requires additional layers of diligence, including, perhaps, a detailed discussion between the CEO and CFO. This might get to 85 or 90 percent accuracy.

A company's audited financial statements that appear in its annual report need to be as accurate as possible. But even greater rigor is required for an information memorandum (IM) being issued to potential investors in your company. Every number that appears in an IM has to be checked and cross-checked, verified by multiple sources, and audited to within an inch of its life.

The risk associated with an imperfect outcome should drive your view on its required accuracy, and therefore how many layers of excellence you need to apply. But no individual is looking to create perfection, even in the most demanding and high-risk process.

3. Demand outputs in draft form to reinforce an iterative approach.

An iterative approach is common in agile organizations, which rely on the principle of starting with a rough outline of something first, before refining it in progressive revisions. This facilitates input into any initiative at an early stage, enabling cheap and rapid correction of major flaws or inconsistencies. It implies an evolutionary cycle for any piece of work, instead of relying on a single, all-or-nothing delivery milestone.

Asking your people to share their work in draft form sets the expectation that they shouldn't be afraid to produce work which is incomplete or ill-formed, and to subject this work to the scrutiny of others. You need to create the expectation that you're happy for a deliverable to be as rough as guts when you first see it, and then refine it with each iteration—but not past the point of diminishing returns.

Several years ago, one of my executives, Melissa, was doing a major piece of strategy work. When I asked how long it would be before the strategy was fully developed, she told me it would be three months. My response? "That's awesome. Three months is fine for the end result, but I'm setting another meeting two weeks from today so that I can look at your first draft."

To say that Melissa was shocked would be an understatement, but it achieved the desired result. I told her that I didn't really care if the draft was nothing more than a few scratchings on the back of a napkin. The objective was to get a look at her early thinking and make any necessary adjustments sooner rather than later. It also broke down her belief in the necessity of perfection by sending a very clear cultural signal: *If the boss is OK with seeing ill-formed output, you don't have to be afraid to involve him in the process when you need to.*

Make no mistake, the final product has to be excellent, and it has to meet the high standard you're setting. But on the way to that finished product, there's a lot of scope to benefit from the iterative approach.

4. **Inspect outputs intermittently to reinforce progress.**
When any major initiative has long delivery time frames, it's important to encourage and reinforce progress at regular milestones. You want to be confident that everything is on track, so you don't get any nasty surprises when it's already too late to take corrective action.

The process starts with the draft work that's delivered for inspection at the earliest sensible opportunity, and then carries through regular, event-driven checkpoints that allow you and your team to retain momentum.

A lot of productive interaction takes place at these milestones, which are a perfect opportunity for coaching and feedback. The language you use here is all-important: you want your people to get the sense of forward momentum that keeps them committed to the excellence-over-perfection mindset. A phrase that I used many times each day: *That's good enough!* You want your people to keep moving forward, make some decisions, and talk to you if they hit any issues or obstacles they can't handle.

HONING YOUR BULLSHIT DETECTOR

You can't unlock true value until you move the culture of your organization to focus on value delivery, above all else. Doing this requires a whole new language, which will feel foreign to your people at first, so don't be surprised at the lengths to which they'll go to drag you back into old ways of working.

You'll need to be able to interrogate information (and people) to get a true picture of what's really going on. The technical term for this is a *bullshit detector*, and it has two distinct parts: first, the ability to ask the right questions, and second, the ability to listen to and synthesize the answers.

I've worked with many executives who either don't possess this skill or choose not to employ it. If you want to understand what value will be derived from any investment of your organization's resources, you need to be able to ask probing questions in the right forums to draw out people's honest opinions.

The skill to listen, synthesize, and redirect can only be developed and refined over a long period of time. It relies on a combination of intellectual capacity and emotional intelligence. But you can improve the quality of your bullshit detector almost immediately by asking better questions. Here are a few common questions that you can adapt to really home in on where the value lies:

Question 1: If we invest the organization's resources into this work, how big is the payback?

Regardless of whether you're chasing financial or non-financial value, it's important to continually reinforce the concept that any investment of resources has to have a clearly defined value outcome. How much value does this work deliver? Not only does this help your people to focus on value creation as the principal consideration for everything they do, but it also paints a clear picture of the *relative* benefit between potential investments you may be considering.

Question 2: Where will the value from this work materialize?

If you're to deliver value from every allocation of organizational resources that you make, you need to know where to look for that value. Too often we *assume* that value will come from something that appears logical.

For example, if you have a team working on a process reengineering initiative, it sounds like that should create value. But it all depends on where your focus goes. Many leaders see the ultimate outcome simply as the implementation of that process. But the new process means nothing *per se*, unless it results in higher-value outcomes for the business: improved efficiency, better safety, increased productivity.

That's one reason why you should never invest your organization's resources without a clear view to a value outcome. *Will we see the value realized in improved asset performance? Will it lower the cost of our operations? Will our people experience fewer injuries as a result of our hazard reduction work? Will our seasonal discounting reduce customer turnover?*

Question 3: When will I see the value from this work?

It's important to understand the time lag between work being completed and the value actually dropping into the bucket. Why? Because any value that's promised has to be baked into future targets and key performance indicators (KPIs). If one of your people makes a commitment that costs will be reduced in a certain area by 10 percent as a result of a project they undertake, that budget item has to be reduced by 10 percent going forward. Understanding timing is crucial if the new targets are to be achievable and rational.

Question 4: Who's accountable for ensuring that this value is captured?

The person who's accountable for delivering a piece of work may not necessarily be the person who's ultimately accountable for capturing the potential value that the work has unlocked.

For example, many large organizations have centralized procurement functions. These teams are accountable for delivering better value contracts with suppliers: the balance of price, quality, service, and risk. However, the procurement team doesn't necessarily manage the contracts they execute; quite often these contracts are administered by line managers in the field. Who's responsible for ensuring the value is delivered? The line managers. They control the ordering and spending habits of their people on a day-to-day basis, and they're the ones who hold the levers for improved supplier performance.

Question 5: Are all the elements of this project critical to delivering the value?

Just because a particular project is deemed to be high value doesn't mean that every proposed activity in the project is necessary to deliver that value.

A good example of this is an investment in the periodic maintenance of a power station. The project itself is undoubtedly critical. If the asset is to perform reliably and provide maximum operational availability, you have to invest. But what's *the right amount* to spend? Can I achieve the same level of operational performance even if I eliminate certain pieces of work that the engineers have requested? If I'm looking purely at asset performance as the value driver, then many lower-level work items can be removed, increasing the value of the investment (spending less, but still delivering the same outcome).

Question 6: If you could ask me for one thing to increase the value of your initiative, what would it be?

This is a great question (and a rather simple one) to ensure your people are thinking about what the key drivers of value are in their work program. You'll also learn a lot about how they perceive value by listening carefully to their answer. Have they asked you for something that will create additional value, or just something that will make them feel more comfortable or make their lives easier?

Question 7: If you could only deliver three of your 20 proposed projects, which three would you choose?

Once again, this question goes to making better choices about where to invest resources. When asked in this way, it forces your people to make choices that they would not otherwise consider. Earlier in this chapter we looked at value ranking, and how this discipline forces your people to place a relative priority on every piece of work based on its potential value. This question helps to keep the value ranking focus at the front of everyone's minds.

Question 8: If everything goes exactly to plan, does this solve our core problem?

Quite often, the work we do and the investments we make only address the symptoms of a problem. Particularly when there's a major disruption or crisis, we move quickly to recover, only to have the situation arise again in the future. We're just kicking the can down the road for a later encounter.

This isn't to say we shouldn't invest in short-term solutions that resolve an immediate issue: it's often unavoidable. But we need to understand the difference between investing in a stop-gap measure, and actually resolving an issue once and for all. I'd be prepared to invest significantly more for the latter.

Question 9: How much analysis have you undertaken on the downside risks?

Every investment proposal, business case, and funding requirement that I've ever had the pleasure of reading suffers from optimism bias. People tend to exaggerate, sometimes wildly, the upside benefits and underrate the downside risks. Probing the downside is an essential discipline in pressure-testing any potential investment.

This primary question opens the door to a vast array of subordinate questions that'll help you to understand the risks that might prevent you from successfully capturing value. For example: *What happens to our export demand if the exchange rate increases above the high end of our assumed range? How much would the ultimate value be affected if weather delays extended the construction period by an additional two months? How low would sales have to be for this new product to become a loss-maker?*

Question 10: Is this expenditure really unavoidable?

You'll often hear that certain investments are unavoidable. Apart from investments that are imposed either by law or regulation, this is almost never the case. In my early chief information officer roles, I was often confronted with investments that were couched as nonnegotiable.

Notwithstanding my personal dislike for having a gun held to my head, there are always options when presented with a compulsory proposition. For example: *You tell me we have no choice but to replace this software because the vendor is withdrawing support at the end of the year. But have you considered the possibility of negotiating an extended support arrangement until we choose to upgrade? Have you analyzed the downside risk of remaining on an unsupported version for a short period of time? Are we sure we even want to continue using this software; what other newer, better alternatives are available in the market now?*

There are almost always choices you can make to improve the value proposition of even a mandatory investment, so probe accordingly.

Finally: The Killer Question

The object of this whole exercise is to shift the culture of your team to focus on delivering value, not just working hard. If you're the only person who truly believes this, you'll be pushing shit uphill every day. It's exhausting.

I came across a killer question quite accidentally a few years ago when running a leadership workshop for the top 50 leaders in my company. In my frustration at the absence of value thinking in the team (and these were my *best* people), I found a question that aligned the interests of the company with the interests of each individual, and shone a light on the path to value:

If I told you that you only had one year left in this organization, and that you then had to go and find a new job, what are the one or two key things you'd like to put on your résumé to ensure that you're as attractive as possible to a new employer?

This breakthrough question helps to shift the thinking from being busy with activity to actually delivering tangible value. It's amazing how often this lines up with the highest-value outcomes for the organization.

As you develop your bullshit detector to make it more accurate and sensitive, remember that your objective is to shift the culture. You're looking for your people to move in the right direction, even if those moves are clumsy and imperfect at first. That's why you always need to reward early attempts at desired behavior. What gets measured gets managed, and what gets rewarded gets done.

CUTTING THROUGH THE BULLSH!T

Gaining a deep understanding of what creates value in your context is your ticket to play. Once you have this, the difficult leadership work begins. How do you focus only on the most valuable things? How do you communicate this value to your people? How do you root out and kill low-value work?

For each of the following questions, rate yourself (on a scale of 1 to 10) before you move on to the next chapter. This will give you greater insight into what stands between you and your ability to deliver *real* value for your stakeholders.

1. How well do you understand what creates the most value at the organizational level?

1   2   3   4   5   6   7   8   9   10

2. How easy is it to understand your work program, and to communicate the value it delivers?

1   2   3   4   5   6   7   8   9   10

73

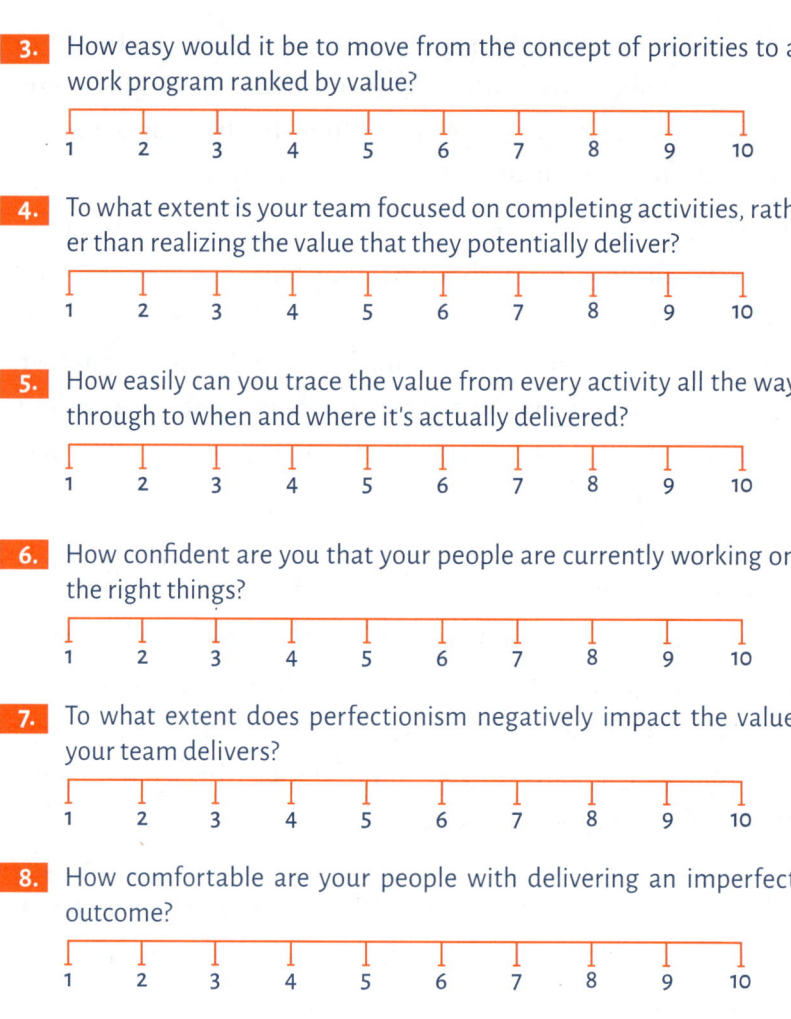

3. How easy would it be to move from the concept of priorities to a work program ranked by value?

1 2 3 4 5 6 7 8 9 10

4. To what extent is your team focused on completing activities, rather than realizing the value that they potentially deliver?

1 2 3 4 5 6 7 8 9 10

5. How easily can you trace the value from every activity all the way through to when and where it's actually delivered?

1 2 3 4 5 6 7 8 9 10

6. How confident are you that your people are currently working on the right things?

1 2 3 4 5 6 7 8 9 10

7. To what extent does perfectionism negatively impact the value your team delivers?

1 2 3 4 5 6 7 8 9 10

8. How comfortable are your people with delivering an imperfect outcome?

1 2 3 4 5 6 7 8 9 10

9. How easy would it be to use the value questions in this chapter to begin to shift the current team culture?

1 2 3 4 5 6 7 8 9 10

CHAPTER 3

HANDLE
CONFLICT

THE BULLSH!T WE BELIEVE

Have you ever heard the expression *happy workers are productive workers?* It sounds like it should be true, but it's not necessarily the case. It's a common mistake to make, though, as we often misinterpret correlation as causation.

Although being happy and being productive might be *correlated*, there's no evidence to suggest that being happy *causes* someone to be productive. Sometimes, happy workers are just... happy. There could be any number of reasons for this. Perhaps the job is really cruisy or offers great benefits. The friendships in the team might make it a fun place to work. The management might let everyone take a half-day on Fridays for an offsite team bonding session over paintball. It certainly doesn't follow that this team will be productive.

But if you're a weak leader, it's incredibly convenient to maintain the belief that leadership is all about keeping your people happy: it gives you a perfect excuse to avoid confrontation, to procrastinate on difficult conversations, and to let your people behave and perform however they choose... *I can't risk upsetting my people, it might demotivate them.*

This is just rationalization. The ability to handle conflict is a core leadership capability, without which a leader will eventually fail. Hiding behind the platitude of keeping people happy, regardless of how they perform, how they behave, or the choices they make, is a recipe for mediocrity and poor culture in your team.

Conflict aversion affects everything you do as a leader. If you can't handle conflict, confidently and competently, it will prevent you from achieving anything near the results that are possible.

Every great leader knows how to handle conflict, to the point that it becomes a differentiating strength. Although this seems almost counterintuitive, the best leaders develop a *preference* for tackling conflict situations head-on (which they do with confidence and ease) rather than avoiding them.

Forget pandering to your people. Instead, you should work to understand what's at the core of your conflict aversion so that you can overcome your fears and not be held back by misplaced and destructive rationalization. //

RESPECT BEFORE POPULARITY

Casey Stengel, the revered Major League Baseball manager, once said, "The secret of [leading] people is to keep the guys who hate you away from the guys who are still undecided." Very droll, but he makes his point beautifully. If you choose to put your hand up for a leadership role, not being liked simply comes with the territory.

Every day when I walked into my company as CEO, I knew that 5 percent of the people hated me for no apparent reason—my haircut, my smile, my tie…whatever. I'm sure there were plenty more who hated me with good reason. The simple fact is that not everyone is going to like you, and you can't worry about it, you can't agonize over it, and you certainly can't change it.

That's why the leader's mantra is really quite simple: *Respect before popularity*. Popularity doesn't matter, but respect does. Don't get me wrong, we all love to be loved, but this can't be our primary goal, because it will prevent us from ever achieving our potential, and it will hold our people and organization back.

Many years ago, I took on an executive role in a business that was on the brink of major change. My incoming brief? To prepare a division of this business to make it commercially viable for a privatization transaction by listing on the Australian Securities Exchange (ASX).

This business was dysfunctional, to say the least, and I had to make some pretty tough decisions on strategy, structure, and people. The workforce had relied on the labor unions to protect them from market forces, and had successfully resisted any moves by management over the years to improve performance. Eventually, the organization was driven to a place of complacency and incompetence, notwithstanding the fact that there were some incredibly talented and hardworking individuals scattered throughout the business.

As I started to make changes (with a level of fervor and commitment that appeared to be completely foreign to my people), the forces of evil, as I affectionately referred to them, fought back with all the ferocity of an angry weasel defending her kits. This resulted in a well-orchestrated smear campaign, the likes of which I'd not previously encountered.

Every week the unions concocted a new story to attack my credibility, my intentions, and my competence. Because these stories played to the existing worldview of the majority of my people, guess what happened? They believed the rumors, no matter how outlandish, and thought I was there for one purpose only: to relieve them of their secure, well-paid, undemanding jobs.

Although I could have spent a lot of time and energy worrying about this, I didn't. This was an entirely predictable, if not entirely welcome, part of the job I'd taken on. If I was to successfully move the people and organization forward, it would get worse before it got better.

But move it forward I did.

I had countless conversations with senior managers and opinion leaders to explain why things had to be different, and what they needed to do to be successful in the new paradigm.

These conversations were always tough, because I needed to show people who'd become complacent about their work environment that change was not optional. Conflict.

I set clear standards for performance and behavior that, for decades, the leadership of the organization had simply chosen to avoid, instead settling for breathtaking mediocrity. Over time, people tend to believe that they're performing to an acceptable standard because the feedback they're given (or not given) convinces them so. Hearing the new kid on the block say that this was no longer good enough, and that they had to lift to a higher standard, was anathema to their fundamental belief system. Conflict.

I put consequences in place when people chose not to meet the standards, and I removed many well-respected, experienced, and knowledgeable people from the company. This was tricky, because long-standing employees generally have broad and deep networks within the business and support in places that might surprise you. Knowing that change requires a critical mass of senior leaders who truly get it, and will work with the same intensity toward the right goals as I would myself, made these decisions easy. But decisions like this inevitably draw opposition, both passive and active, throughout the business. Conflict.

I hired new people as exemplars of the behavior and performance I was trying to instill in the business. And yes, I got some of these hires wrong, further reinforcing my incompetence in the minds of the silent majority. When you drive to lift the standard and change a culture, many people will be watching intently, just waiting for you to fail. Conflict.

All of these actions, which I consciously chose to take with an uncommon level of gusto, created conflict. But the only other option I had was to leave this corporate division exactly as it was, and be satisfied with a substandard outcome. For me, this wasn't an option.

Ultimately, the organization went through one of the most successful IPOs that the ASX had ever seen. My division was only a small part of this success, but I know exactly how much value was created and how many people's lives changed as a result. And it was completely worth it! Every single conflict situation that I willingly put myself into brought the organization closer to victory.

As a leader, you sometimes have to drag people kicking and screaming to a better world. But if you struggle to put respect before popularity, you'll subconsciously choose not to invest the time, effort, and personal risk required to do so.

Overcoming our subconscious drivers can be learned, but it requires discipline. That's why each day I reflect on the things that I should have done but chose to avoid. It takes only 15 minutes, but it's probably the most important part of every day for me—holding myself to account for doing what needs to be done and ensuring that I look inside myself to uncover the reasons for any hesitation. More often than not, it's the avoidance of conflict or the fear of not being liked that holds me back. The need for acceptance is programmed into our DNA and controls us all to some extent.

A leader learns how to let go of the need for acceptance and popularity in preference for the deep respect that is the bedrock of successful leadership.

CONFLICT AVERSION HOLDS US BACK

Just think for a moment. In your leadership career to date, which scenarios, events, or circumstances have you found the most challenging? Chances are, the root cause of your discomfort is a conflict you found yourself in that you would have rather avoided.

When this happens, it doesn't just affect your performance, but your confidence, self-esteem, and job satisfaction as well. It also affects the people you lead, who have a reasonable expectation that you can handle the rigors of your job!

Let's have a quick look at the key areas where conflict aversion will attempt to derail you.

Difficult Conversations

Personal conflict with another individual is often the most difficult of all conflicts. There's nowhere to run and nowhere to hide—just the expectation that you'll handle the situation competently and professionally.

Often these take place one-on-one, in small rooms and offices, with no support, no guidance, and no reward at the end. A conversation like this can challenge your commitment to the *respect before popularity* principle like no other situation can.

Building a High-Performing Team

If you can't pull the basic leadership levers of *challenging*, *coaching*, and *confronting* your people, it's impossible to build a high-performing team. Conflict comes with the territory.

Building a great team starts with hiring the best individuals you possibly can, and then challenging them to lift to a higher standard. This is essential before you can even think about the tough bits (like having to manage nonperformers out of the organization).

Negotiating

Even the friendliest and most relaxed negotiations incorporate some level of conflict as the parties wrestle to claim value. How do you expect to achieve great results if you can't absorb the shock of the conflict while remaining calm, rational, and present? I see many senior people who know all the right negotiating techniques but are let down by their temperament and their inability to sit comfortably in a conflict situation.

Decision-Making

The higher up you go, the more impactful your decisions become. The more layers of people you have below you, the less likely your team is to understand your rationale for making any given decision. At the most senior levels of an organization, it's virtually impossible to make a decision that's universally popular. That's just the way it is.

The unwillingness to be seen in an unfavorable light by the team stops many smart, competent, experienced leaders from making the right decisions in a timely fashion.

Contributing to the Broader Group

Even something as simple as expressing your views and opinions in a group meeting can generate conflict, and we've all felt the disappointment of leaving a meeting having not said what was on our minds.

Wouldn't it be phenomenal if we could put aside our fear of conflict, and instead focus our efforts on doing the best we possibly could for the people we lead? Focusing outwardly (on our team) rather than inwardly (on ourselves) is the key to overcoming conflict aversion.

I've been privileged to see the life-changing impact that a leader can have on another individual if they're stretched and supported to exceed their self-imposed limitations. However, you can't build your people's confidence and self-esteem until you master your own impulse to avoid conflict.

TRUST AND CONFLICT

Once we accept the need to overcome our fear of conflict, it's much easier to take the next step: making the necessary changes to bring out the best in our people. Trust plays a critical role in this. If you're going to embark on any difficult conversation with another human, there's a liberating principle that will make this easier: if someone trusts and respects you, there's *nothing* you can't say to them.

Trust is the bedrock of leadership, and it's a two-way street—you need to trust your people, while at the same time earning their trust.

There's a number of critical leadership behaviors that drive trust. Working out how to incorporate these behaviors—in the right measure—into your leadership repertoire is different for everyone. Whilst we each have a unique leadership fingerprint that no other leader possesses, incorporating the behaviors that build trust into our own leadership persona will only enhance our performance. That is, providing it's congruent and authentic!

Over my career, I've found that there are seven basic behaviors that most contribute to building a strong level of trust:

| Openness and Transparency

It's important to show your people who you are, and to be open about your thoughts, actions, and decisions. Obviously, you won't be able to tell them everything, but if you can be clear about your intentions, goals, and expectations, this quickly builds trust (as long as you eat your own dog food). If your words and actions are consistent, then you're really just thinking out loud.

| Consistency

Erratic bosses can be a real problem. If you're unpredictable, your people will spend more time trying to guess what pleases you, rather than delivering the value they should. Delay in delivering outcomes is compounded by rework, as people try to meet your ever-evolving expectations. If your people know what to expect from you, and how you'll react under normal circumstances, they can just get on with it.

Fallibility

No one is perfect, so we shouldn't pretend we are. Fortunately, my career path solved this for me: as I've worked in so many different industries, I could never hide behind my industry knowledge, and I frequently had people working under me whose knowledge of the business far exceeded mine. I had no choice but to appear fallible because (self-evidently) I was. But I had to be comfortable with this, and I had to win my team's confidence by demonstrating that, despite my lack of knowledge in one area, I more than adequately compensated for this in other areas. This had the serendipitous effect of not only building trust, but also developing the team's confidence in my unique capabilities.

Truth

Ah, that Jack Nicholson line from the movie *A Few Good Men*. "You want the truth? You can't handle the truth!" Well, you'd be surprised what people can actually handle. I've found that protracted uncertainty is way more destabilizing for a team than a hard truth. The unfolding of the COVID-19 pandemic graphically displayed this, as countries and businesses struggled to understand its implications.

People hate uncertainty way more than bad news, because at least with bad news they can move forward. When it comes to people, truth will always eventually win out. Deceptive behavior is trust suicide.

Absence of Self-Interest

If you're in it for yourself, your people will never be in it for you. *Ever.* Showing that you only make decisions for the greater good, not for personal gain, has two important ramifications: it builds the trust of your people, and it sets a high bar for their own behavior.

| Courage

Many leaders tend to follow the path of least resistance: they do what's easy and expedient. Having the courage to do the right thing, when it needs to be done—every time—simply because it's right, will build your people's trust. They'll see that you're not afraid to respectfully challenge others, even the CEO or chairman, if you really believe in something.

| Having Your People's Backs

Critical to building trust is that people know you'll give them credit where it's due, and you'll protect them when they fail. Arnold H. Glasow said, "A good leader takes a little more than his share of the blame, a little less than his share of the credit."

We have to be careful with this one, though: having your people's backs doesn't mean that they're absolved of accountability for their behavior and performance. What it does mean is that as long as they operate with the right intent and values, and don't go out of bounds by ignoring your specific direction, you should provide air cover for them.

In my previous example of the pre-IPO turnaround, trust played a major part. It's fair to say that I never really got to the stage where I felt I had won the trust of the majority of the people: they simply weren't close enough to me to cross that chasm, and the forces of evil were ever-present in their psyches. *Respect before popularity*, right?

However, I did manage to win the trust of the majority of *leaders* throughout the layers of my division, and here's why: I ensured that they actually bought into the overall purpose of the change and believed in the benefits it would bring. I didn't sugarcoat how difficult and painful the journey would be. I showed them that I wasn't afraid to take on challenges, no matter how difficult. I demonstrated every day that my decisions were driven by pursuing the best interests of the team and the organization, not simply taking the easy route, or operating in my own narrow self-interest. And I didn't take a backward step, no matter how much pressure was placed on me to do so.

This trust gave the leaders below me the confidence to follow my lead, and good things started to happen as they built upon that foundation.

THE PSYCHOLOGY OF FEEDBACK

In the quest to overcome your conflict aversion so that you can handle even the most charged situations with confidence, you need to start with the one-on-one interactions with your people. If you can master the conflict that arises in feedback conversations, in time you'll be able to hold any conversation, no matter how difficult, without even thinking about it. It will become an unconscious competence.

These conversations are the hardest: they're held with the people whom, arguably, you have the strongest relationships with. They're the people with whom you'll feel the gravitational pull of belonging and identity. Initiating difficult performance conversations puts this at risk. But if you can manage to overcome this, the ability to handle any other type of conflict (team conflict, negotiation, decision-making, etc.) will quickly follow.

Then why do we find it so difficult? Well, for a start, leaders who model this behavior are few and far between. The scarcity of strong leaders leaves a void of practical examples for us to draw upon. And if your boss isn't regularly having difficult conversations, it's extremely unlikely that she will demand it of you. Ultimately, no one really knows whether you're doing it or not (except your people, of course).

Eventually, it'll be obvious through poor team performance, but even then it's often seen as a victimless crime—there's always another excuse to blame for a failure.

I've heard every excuse ever invented from leaders trying to convince themselves that a difficult conversation isn't necessary. These rationalizations can take hold of the most committed leader. *I shouldn't criticize my people—what if it demotivates them?... I don't really have enough evidence or examples—what if they disagree with my assessment of the situation?... What if I haven't set them up for success (maybe it's my fault)?... Am I too demanding? Maybe I'm asking too much of them?... What if it escalates into conflict?... If I leave them alone, perhaps they'll improve over time?...* Or, my favorite, *They've never had a leader like me before, so they'll be better under my leadership*—rationalization and arrogance, all in the same sentence!

Whatever our excuses, we need to move past these if we have any aspirations of being competent, let alone exceptional leaders.

But the dread and fear we harbor about these situations is self-reinforcing. If we're fearful of a conversation, we'll handle it poorly, and it won't go well. This reinforces our underlying belief that having difficult conversations is hard, and we don't like them. From then on, we'll naturally avoid those conversations like the plague, all the while rationalizing why we don't *really* need to hold them, or that they're not a priority compared to our other busywork.

Let's face it, if we don't do it, we don't improve. So when we finally come to the point where a difficult conversation is simply unavoidable, guess what happens? It goes badly again. Predictably.

This is 90 percent will and 10 percent skill, so let's focus on the 90 percent. How do you establish the right mindset to willingly take on these difficult conversations whenever they need to be held? It's a matter of having the right lens to look through—taking the focus off yourself and what it might mean for you, and putting this focus onto your people.

Here are the five lenses through which to change your perspective on holding difficult feedback conversations:

1. You have a duty of care to your people.

Part of being a leader is that you're charged with the mental, physical, and emotional well-being of your people when they're under your care. You need to take this obligation seriously, and ensure you let your people know what your expectations are and how they're measuring up to those expectations.

Because safety was an ever-present threat in the types of industrial organizations I worked in, setting standards for behavior and performance around the things that kept my people safe was critical. Had I not taken that duty of care seriously, the outcomes may have been very different. Putting the focus on the physical well-being of my people every day was a great antidote to any temptation I may have had to avoid a difficult conversation.

2. You can't get results from a subpar team.

Leaders get results, first and foremost. If you aren't facing difficult performance conversations when they're required, your team will be substandard, by definition. I don't know any member of a nonperforming team who's actually happy: there's nothing more demoralizing to a good performer than watching poor performance go unchecked.

Difficult conversations are part and parcel of lifting team standards and performance, and avoiding these simply leaves you with whatever level of behavior and performance was there before you turned up. Value doesn't ever magically appear. Nothing happens unless a leader makes it happen.

3. Your people deserve the opportunity to improve.

I never cease to be amazed at how many people I've led over the years who, even in their 40s or 50s, have never been made aware of an obvious behavioral or performance issue. They've never worked for a leader with the courage and self-lessness to give them the feedback that could have changed the trajectory of their career, or even their life.

I've also seen the incredible joy that people experience when they overcome a limiting belief and are given the wherewithal to change. Feedback is truly a gift, and those who choose to listen can make changes that would never have been possible without their leader's willingness to have the hard conversation. But this is risky—not everyone wants to hear these messages, and conflict abounds in feedback conversations.

4. Everyone knows the strong and weak performers.

We sometimes think that others can't see what we can see, so we go ostrich, burying our heads in the sand. Just know that everyone can see the strong and weak performers, and you can't fool anyone. Think of *The Emperor's New Clothes*.

If you don't deal with individual underperformance, your team performance suffers, the good people eventually leave, and you end up with a reputation as a weak leader. It's both as difficult and as simple as that. And in that scenario, everyone loses.

5. If worse comes to worst, you need to know you've done everything possible.

People choose how they behave and perform when they come into work each day. They decide how much effort and commitment to give, how much time to spend counting the likes on their latest selfie, and how much time to spend gossiping around the watercooler. Still, as the leader you need to be confident that, if push comes to shove and you need to remove someone from the organization, you've done everything you possibly could have to help them succeed. If not, you'll never be comfortable with your decision.

Many leaders over the years have approached me to say that they needed to remove a nonperformer from their team. In many cases, when I asked if they felt as though they'd given sufficient feedback to the individual in question, the answer was *no*. Without this, even a thinly disguised restructure to remove an individual (with a bag of money to assuage your guilt) won't make you feel any better.

So every time you get that little niggle in the back of your head telling you that you may have avoided a difficult conversation, read through these lenses. Get yourself in the frame of mind that says, *I'm a strong leader who's focused on doing the best I possibly can for my team and the organization. Besides, it's what I get paid for, and I have strong professional pride.* When this is your mantra, you'll find that one of the five lenses perfectly resolves your dilemma.

The five lenses should ultimately enable you to move yourself to action, to put your fear and discomfort aside, and to take on the most difficult of leadership conversations. If this doesn't entice you to act in the face of conflict, then you may need to rethink your career aspirations as a leader!

DELIVERING FEEDBACK COMPETENTLY

Having established that difficult conversations are 90 percent will, the 10 percent skill is still important. It all starts with the leadership dialogue. This is the day-to-day interaction that you have with your people. The objective is to build a trusting relationship, and it's here that you'll become accustomed to having nonconfrontational conversations, and to know your people personally, at an appropriate level. Your goal is to develop a relationship where you're friendly, but not friends.

Building social friendships with your people can have unintended consequences. In a work context, your friends are likely to take advantage of your good nature, and you're likely to make inappropriate concessions for them, even if only subconsciously. Others in your team will see this and become disgruntled—they'll see you as a leader who plays favorites, and it undermines their faith in the meritocracy.

If you have regular interactions with your people and give them consistent direction, they'll soon gain confidence in your leadership style, and they'll start to open up to you. Using the leadership dialogue to set clear expectations is where the foundations for high performance are laid.

It's mastery of difficult conversations, however, that determines how effective your leadership can be. It's a skill that you need to learn, practice, and develop, just as you would any other. The difficulty is that it takes emotional and psychological discipline, and a strong commitment to your role as a leader.

At the start, you can gain enormous confidence by carefully scripting your conversations. If at first you're not confident, then you should overprepare. Perhaps seek guidance from a person in your organization who you think has mastered this skill. Practice until you're confident that you can do the person on the other side of the table justice. But whatever you do, give it your due attention.

A good feedback conversation has seven key elements:

| Clarity

You may find it hard to resist the temptation to raise a litany of points to prove that your feedback is warranted. Raising too many issues at once is a trap we can easily fall into. Make sure there is *one* key message that you want the individual to take from the conversation, and deliver it with extreme clarity.

For example: *I've noticed that when you're faced with questioning in meetings, as you were in yesterday's business review presentation, you shut down and refuse to entertain debate.*

| Balance

Put that key message into the context of the person's overall performance. Make sure that they understand whether the issue at hand is consistent with their overall performance, or an anomaly that needs to be addressed. And don't use the shit sandwich technique—*you're awesome/this is rubbish/but don't worry, you're awesome.* Some leaders use this to soften the difficult message (the shit) and make themselves feel better by placing it between two beautiful, soft pieces of white bread. Lose the bread—it makes the whole process feel disingenuous, and the message will be lost.

For example: *Although your overall performance is excellent, you often have a tendency to disregard expert advice. This may hold you back if you don't nip it in the bud.*

| Tangibility

Bring the point to life with specific examples that clearly demonstrate the behavioral or performance issue you're highlighting.

The more specific and timely you can make this, the easier the conversation will be. On many occasions I've asked an individual to join me immediately after a meeting to offer some feedback or guidance on something I observed them doing or saying during the meeting. These are relatively easy conversations to have.

For example: *The way you spoke to Keith wasn't acceptable for a leader at any level, let alone yours. It wasn't just the language you used, but your aggressive tone and posture as well.*

Mutuality

It needs to be a conversation, not a sermon. Give the person the opportunity to talk, ask questions, clarify, and put their own perspectives into the mix. Oh, and make sure you listen to them intently, otherwise it's just a thinly disguised lecture.

Learn to ask leading questions.

For example: *Do you think there's any value to be found in the comments and observations of your peers?*

Criticality

Make sure you're clear about the criticality that the individual should place on your feedback. Are you suggesting a few tweaks to fine-tune their performance? Is it a major concern? Is it a potential show-stopper that could ultimately impact their employment? Be clear.

For example: *This isn't a big deal, but if you can learn to do this, it'll improve your leadership capability even further.* Or: *This is a show-stopper. If you don't get this under control pretty quickly, you can't be successful in this role.*

Accountability

What do you need the person to take accountability for working on, so that they can improve? Once again, this requires a high degree of specificity.

For example: *We know what needs to change, so why don't you think about how you might approach this, and come back to me in a couple of days with a plan for how you might be able to fix it. I'll make half an hour for you on Thursday.*

| Support

What will you do to support them, to help them reach the required standard? What resources, time, and guidance are you prepared to invest in their development? (The answer is not always *whatever it takes*—be judicious about this.)

For example: *I'm here to support you to give you the best chance to resolve this issue, but it's really going to be up to you to decide if you're willing to put the effort into make the change. I can only do so much.*

Focusing on the other person will liberate you to be your best when holding a difficult conversation. From there, it's all about frequency and repetition. You just need to do enough of this until it starts to feel comfortable. There's no other way, which is why the leaders who avoid this work never master it and often spend their whole careers doing jobs they hate.

It's important to realize that these conversations are not just for people who are underperforming. Even your best performers benefit from specific, targeted, direct feedback.

I recall a young executive who worked for me recently. Tony was a standout performer. He was intelligent, professionally competent, had great values and integrity, and set high standards for himself and his team. He was a dream employee in a critical role, whom I relied upon to do an outstanding job (which he did).

One day in a board meeting, I picked up on a minor behavioral issue. After presenting a paper to the board almost flawlessly, he was asked a series of questions, which he didn't handle particularly well.

Immediately after the meeting, I called Tony into my office. After commending him on his presentation of the paper, I asked if he noticed anything about the questions from the directors. He immediately confessed that he didn't really understand the questions, so he chose to simply reiterate the points he'd already made as part of his presentation.

I was able to coach him on other possible responses. "Perhaps next time, ask for clarification. Maybe throw the question to the CEO if you're unsure...or, sometimes, you don't even attempt to answer the question. It's perfectly fine to say 'I hadn't thought about that, but it's a great question. I'll need to take it away and get back to you with an answer.'"

I was able to have a conversation with a high performer that's likely to build his capability and performance to even greater heights. Not all difficult conversations are particularly difficult.

CONFLICT IN NEGOTIATIONS

Most executives, at some point in their careers, study negotiation techniques. They learn about zones of possible agreement, best alternatives to a negotiated agreement, and how to trade terms effectively—skills and tactics. Unfortunately, most never learn about *temperament*. You can learn technique, but if that's all you focus on, you won't excel as a negotiator.

Negotiation is, by its nature, an adversarial construct. Remaining calm and composed in a negotiation is critical to optimizing results, and those who can't command their emotions will lose out. As conflict escalates, I've seen otherwise smart, capable, experienced leaders flounder. When confronted with conflict, they often stop listening and make mistakes, as they can't remain analytical and composed under pressure.

One of the most useful techniques for handling conflict in negotiations is to learn to reframe your emotions. We can experience a range of emotions in high-pressure situations, and many people are slaves to these emotions, allowing them to affect their behavior and, ultimately, their decisions.

The first step in reframing is that you must be *aware* of your emotional responses before you can attempt to manage them. Are there times when you feel yourself getting angry? Frustrated? Fearful? These are normal emotions, driven by triggers deep within us. Although it's virtually impossible to prevent them from welling up inside, we can absolutely learn to manage them.

There are all sorts of reasons why negative emotions flow in high-pressure negotiations. We can feel angry when we perceive that the other party is trying to take advantage of us. We can feel frustrated when they don't understand our position, or confused when we don't understand theirs. We can feel fearful when the balance of the scales seems to be tipping against us.

I realized some years ago that I'm personally triggered by inequity. When I see a counterpart trying to unfairly take a disproportionate share of the available value, I get angry. But the good news is that I'm aware of this, and constantly vigilant of that feeling being triggered.

Irrespective of what triggers each of us, there's one emotion that we can productively use to replace any negative emotion: *curiosity.*

Seeking to understand *why* a counterpart is behaving in a particular way, or saying certain things, can completely displace the negative emotion and set you on a new path—the path of inquisitiveness and discovery.

Once you shift to a position of curiosity, it also has an interesting effect on your perceptions of your counterpart: you intuitively give them the benefit of the doubt (unless, of course, you have evidence to the contrary). If I'm given the choice of ascribing either malice or incompetence to someone's actions, I start with incompetence and work from there. Most often, you'll find that people aren't malicious, but their actions are simply a result of thoughtlessness.

There are some stock questions you can ask yourself whenever confronted with negative emotions to help you reframe them into curiosity.

Question 1: Why is this important to them?

Consider why your counterparts may be particularly focused on a certain issue. This will provide insights into what drives their position, thereby increasing the chances that you can successfully find middle ground. Quite often, the things that are most important to them may not be critical to you, and vice versa. It's only through these lines of questioning and consideration that the potential for mutual value can be discovered.

Question 2: Why do they think this would be acceptable to us?

When you hear a preposterous proposal that seems to taunt you, it's easy to get angry. But it's incredibly powerful to be able to consider what may have driven their statement. Sure, it's possible that they said something just to try to get under your skin, but it's more likely an indication that they fundamentally misunderstand your position, and how you've valued a particular component of the deal.

Question 3: Why are they behaving this way?

Not many leaders learn to master their emotions the way you now will, so always be aware of the struggles that other people in the room are having to keep their negative emotions in check and retain their composure and rationality. Give them the latitude for a response that's not as respectful as you deserve. Instead of becoming indignant, take the opportunity to learn more about their negotiating triggers.

Question 4: What did I just learn from that statement?

Always seek to learn from the cues your counterpart's giving you, both verbal and nonverbal. This requires you to be in the moment, to listen and watch intently, and to remain inquisitive about what you observe. This is how you'll find a path that secures the deal you're hoping for.

As you become more comfortable and proficient with the questioning mindset, you can start to make the questions explicit, rather than implicit.

It can be quite disarming for your counterpart when you ask, for example, "What makes you think that this would be acceptable to us?" It's a very powerful tool to have at your disposal in any negotiating situation.

And yes, there's still technique—but that's not what's going to make you great. Your emotional intelligence and your ability to remain calm and inquisitive in the most adverse, high-pressure conflict situations is what shines through.

CUTTING THROUGH THE BULLSH!T

Because conflict aversion is at the heart of rationalization and avoidance, you need to learn to face your fears if you're ever going to improve. First, you have to pinpoint the situations that you're most likely to avoid, and then commit to willingly put yourself in these situations. This means mustering the courage to push through your fear, anxiety, and discomfort until you don't feel the same level of trepidation.

For each of the following questions, rate yourself (on a scale of 1 to 10) before you move on to the next chapter. This will give you greater insight into what stands between you and your ability to comfortably handle conflict in any situation.

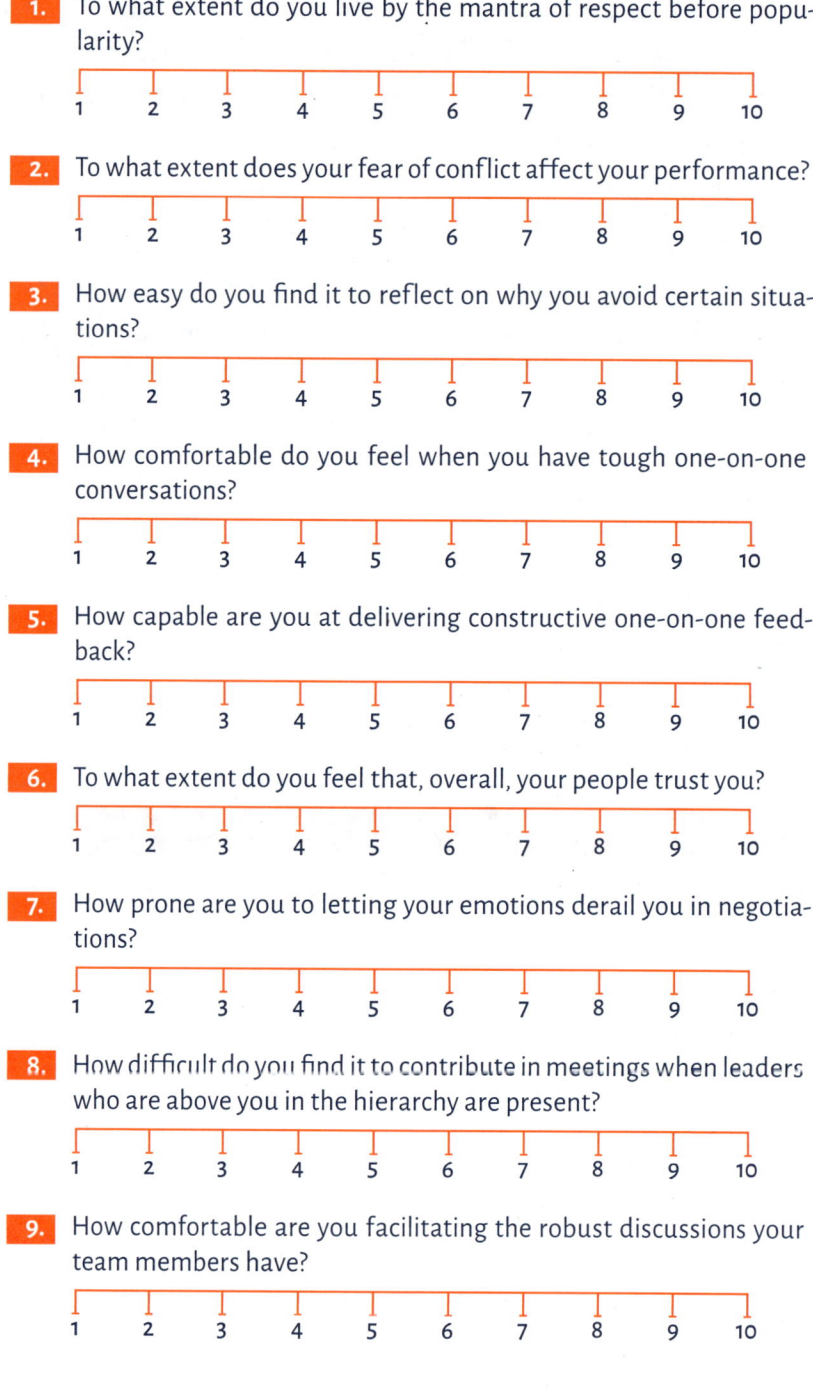

1. To what extent do you live by the mantra of respect before popularity?

   1 2 3 4 5 6 7 8 9 10

2. To what extent does your fear of conflict affect your performance?

   1 2 3 4 5 6 7 8 9 10

3. How easy do you find it to reflect on why you avoid certain situations?

   1 2 3 4 5 6 7 8 9 10

4. How comfortable do you feel when you have tough one-on-one conversations?

   1 2 3 4 5 6 7 8 9 10

5. How capable are you at delivering constructive one-on-one feedback?

   1 2 3 4 5 6 7 8 9 10

6. To what extent do you feel that, overall, your people trust you?

   1 2 3 4 5 6 7 8 9 10

7. How prone are you to letting your emotions derail you in negotiations?

   1 2 3 4 5 6 7 8 9 10

8. How difficult do you find it to contribute in meetings when leaders who are above you in the hierarchy are present?

   1 2 3 4 5 6 7 8 9 10

9. How comfortable are you facilitating the robust discussions your team members have?

   1 2 3 4 5 6 7 8 9 10

CHAPTER 4

BUILD
RESILIENCE

THE BULLSH!T WE BELIEVE

Are you good under pressure? *Really?* We all like to think that we are, but too often there's a yawning gap between our self-perceptions and the reality that the people around us experience. We amplify the problem when we manage to convince ourselves that we *don't* have a problem—and blind ourselves to the consequences of our behavior.

Unfortunately, even if we've mastered the outward appearance of being good under pressure, people can see through the veneer. There are dozens of ways that we unwittingly show people what's really going on for us, and that we're anything but calm. Although many leaders learn to maintain a facade more or less successfully, very few are genuinely calm, rational, and fearless under pressure.

But pressure is precisely the thing that reveals what a leader is truly made of. As the Latin writer Publilius Syrus said, long before the word *resilience* was a thing, "Anyone can hold the helm when the sea is calm."

Too often, we make the mistake of believing our own bullshit: that resilience is just about mustering our game face, so that the people around us can't see the crushing panic we feel inside. But resilience is a lot more than this, and it's not until we learn to control our mental, emotional, and physical state that we can be truly effective leaders in the face of adversity. Once we do, it changes the whole tone of a crisis, the perceptions of the people around us, and the outcomes we can achieve as a result.

The first step in building resilience is to be brutally honest with ourselves about our capacity for handling adversity, and to understand how it impairs our normal behaviors. Only then do we open up to the things we can do to improve. //

THE BALANCED LEADER

As I've grown a little older and wiser, I've become convinced that success in career, business, and life relies on a combination of three foundational capabilities: your raw intelligence, your ability to understand and manage emotions, and your level of resilience. I think of these as the three legs of a stool. If one is underdeveloped, the stool is (at best) unstable or (at worst) unusable. Great leaders learn to integrate these three capabilities, giving them the balance they need to perform competently, no matter the external conditions.

We can do much to improve each of these capabilities (yes, even our IQ), but it's only when we make a deliberate decision to do so that we make any progress. Let's start by taking a closer look at each of the three legs of our success stool.

| Intelligence Quotient (IQ)

The concept of IQ has been around for a long time, and attempts have been made to measure it since the late 19th century. This is about your intellectual horsepower— your capacity to handle complexity and to absorb new concepts readily.

Conventional wisdom says that your IQ can't really be improved. Like an internal combustion engine, once it's built, that's it.

Whether or not that's true, there are a range of ways to improve what I call your *apparent* IQ. By increasing your own knowledge, and better leveraging the capability of others, you'll appear a lot smarter than you otherwise would, and you're more likely to achieve superior results.

I amply demonstrated throughout my career that I didn't have to be the smartest or best at everything—I only had to be excellent at finding the people who were, and to work out how to harness their intellect and expertise. But I first had to be sufficiently self-aware to know the areas where I wasn't strong. That was down to my emotional intelligence, which we'll address shortly.

Continuous learning also played a big part in improving my knowledge, and increasing my apparent IQ. It doesn't take much, other than a little commitment and discipline, to learn a new word each day, but if you do, it will pay you back in multiples.

I love a good Netflix binge as much as the next person, but every day I allocate time to reading things that improve my knowledge, broaden my perspective, and provide insights. *Every* day. But it's also important to remain intellectually skeptical about any information we're served.

Developing your apparent IQ is a worthwhile endeavor, but it's important to realize that, if you've had any success at all in life, you're probably *smart enough*. You must have been able to learn, make decisions, and process information in a changing environment. You don't need to be a genius for most pursuits, and certainly not for leadership—the other two legs of the stool are equally important, and far easier to develop.

| Emotional Quotient (EQ)

I've mentioned emotional intelligence in the preceding chapters, so let's now take a closer look. EQ is a relatively recent concept. It was first formally recognized as a driver of behavioral outcomes as early as the mid-1960s, but it didn't achieve real prominence until the release of Daniel Goleman's book *Emotional Intelligence* in 1995.

EQ is the ability to recognize, manage, and use emotions, and it's equally important in self-management as it is in interacting with others. In my experience, EQ is a more accurate predictor of long-term leadership success than IQ. I've seen many smart leaders fail because they couldn't relate to, connect with, and influence others.

The further you progress along your leadership journey, the more you'll realize how important emotional intelligence actually is. EQ is a prerequisite for developing empathy, the essential ingredient in connecting with others at a meaningful level. Most of the concepts and tools in this book require the ongoing development of your EQ in order to improve as a leader.

In the previous chapter, we looked at having difficult conversations with your people, and handling conflict in negotiations. These are two core leadership capabilities that can't be handled competently without the foundation of a strong EQ. The better you can read the emotional cues of others, the better you can understand them and come up with an appropriate response.

Whenever I hired a senior person to work for me, I'd put them through a comprehensive battery of testing, including intellectual aptitude, critical thinking skills, personality, and emotional intelligence. It was the emotional intelligence result that I paid closest attention to, as a way of calibrating what we'd observed in other phases of the hiring process.

On the one occasion that I ignored a very poor EQ result in an executive's pre-employment testing, it didn't end well. The testing indicated that Nancy's ability to recognize, manage, understand, and use emotions was remedial at best. And despite the litany of achievements in Nancy's CV, the glowing references given by her sponsors, and a competent interview performance, this was definitely a problem.

I realized, a little later than I would have liked, that Nancy simply couldn't deliver results.

Clarity eluded Nancy's team, because she was unable to connect and communicate with them. They often grumbled that they had no idea what she actually wanted them to do. This led to confusion and lack of focus on the core objectives of her portfolio. Everyone muddled along as best they could, in the absence of clearer guidance.

Nancy's lack of EQ also noticeably affected her ability to perform as an executive. In critical meetings, she struggled to read the play. Over the years, she'd learned to say nothing at all rather than expose her lack of emotional connectedness. Even when I provided direct and unambiguous feedback, Nancy rationalized by saying "I'm not like the men—I only speak when I have something to say." That's never going to cut the mustard for a senior executive.

| Adversity Quotient (AQ)

The final piece of the puzzle is resilience. AQ is probably the least known measure of the three, and it has had a lot less academic rigor and scrutiny applied to it than either IQ or EQ. It's critical nonetheless, and it's useful to consider AQ as part of the mental model that constitutes a balanced leader.

In 1997, Paul Stoltz published his book *Adversity Quotient: Turning Obstacles into Opportunities*, formalizing the idea that resilience is a common attribute in successful people. Resilience is often described as perseverance, grit, determination, tenacity, or endurance. All of these terms convey a similar sentiment, and purport to measure the same thing: How well equipped are we to handle the inevitable challenges, setbacks, and disappointments that we experience as we go through life?

For leaders, resilience isn't optional, and we'll see shortly how resilience can make or break a team in times of crisis. Great leaders possess a highly developed AQ, enabling them to perform equally well in crises as they do in the general run of play.

Resilience can be developed simply through being exposed to adversity, and learning to cope with it in all its forms. Leading a team through a crisis is the obvious way to build the muscles of resilience. But adversity isn't always event-driven—it can come in many forms.

The most accelerated period of AQ growth in my life came almost 20 years ago, not as the result of a single event, but a combination of factors that brought adversity into my world.

I'd moved cities to take a chief information officer role with a top-50 ASX-listed mining company, in an industry which I'd not previously worked. That was a pretty steep learning curve to climb, and came with a 60- to 70-hour-week commitment. On top of that, I was living about 60 miles from the office, requiring 12 to 15 hours of commuting time each week.

At the same time, I was going through a divorce, which, although pretty tame in comparison to some of my friends' experiences, placed a heavy emotional burden on me and my two daughters.

It just so happened that I was also studying to receive my MBA (in intensive mode, naturally), doing assignments and preparing for exams whenever I wasn't buried in the other demands.

And just when I thought the load was unbearable, the company I worked for became the target of a semi-hostile takeover. After the takeover completed, I spent the next year working with the new owner to integrate our systems with theirs, restructure and downsize the workforce, and outsource some of the critical support services.

At any point, I could have thrown in the towel, or at least tried to ease back on one of the pressure points. Let's see… no, I couldn't postpone my divorce. What else could I do? Well, the job was the job, and by this stage my career was important to me. *I know, I'll postpone my MBA!*

I have to say, I came pretty close to deferring my MBA studies on several occasions. But it always came back to the same thing, which became my resilience mantra: *If I can't handle the pressure now, then I'd better re-evaluate my life goals. If I can't handle this, then there's no way I'll be able to live the sort of life and have the sort of career I want. This is just preparing me for what lies ahead, so suck it up, cupcake!*

I navigated my way through this, and collapsed in a heap a year or two later, when the merry-go-round stopped spinning. But I came out of that period with an incredible level of confidence that I could handle virtually anything that life threw at me. And since then, I have.

KNOWING YOURSELF

Are you a good driver? If you're like most people, it's likely that you answered *yes*, but do the facts support your self-assessment? Allstate Insurance conducted a survey in 2011 to better understand people's perceptions of their driving skills, and the results were telling.

Almost two-thirds (64 percent) of those surveyed rated their own driving skills as either "excellent" or "very good." Yet when asked to rate their family and friends, only 29 percent gave them the same rating. And when it came to others of the same age group, the number dropped even further. Only 22 percent of the surveyed drivers said that others in their same age group were good drivers. *I'm OK, you're not OK.*

This is a demonstration of the Dunning–Kruger effect, which was named for the two social psychologists who described it in their 1999 study, "Unskilled and Unaware of It." We tend to overestimate our own capabilities, performance, and impact, and underestimate others'. This comes through in people's self-ratings on everything from their academic ability to their competence in investing. A slew of studies show that over 80 percent of people (and sometimes as high as 93 percent) consider themselves to be above average. Statistically, of course, this is impossible.

The technical term for this phenomenon is *illusory superiority* bias, and it factors into many areas of a leader's performance, none more so than the ability to function under pressure.

We often overestimate how well we deal with pressure, even as we look around us at the many leaders who *don't* deal with it particularly well. Let's try to understand a few varieties of poor crisis management.

| The Landmine Leader

Have you ever noticed how some leaders are quick to anger? Some exhibit physiological signs that are relatively subtle. For example, their face may become flushed, or they may adopt a more closed posture and body language than they had before they were triggered. Others, however, are much more demonstrative about their anger, raising their voices and becoming abusive when they're under pressure.

I call them *landmine leaders* because everything can be going along happily until they hit a difficult patch, then they explode without warning. Sometimes it's just a simple raising of the voice, which, let's face it, we've all done. But others go so far as to yell at people, and to take their anger out on inanimate objects.

I've seen a leader throw a chair across his office, smashing the unsuspecting plant pot on the window ledge. I've seen another become verbally abusive to someone three levels below her in the hierarchy, just because he gave an honest answer that she didn't want to hear. This is incredibly detrimental, not just to the individuals in the firing line, but to the team and organization.

When you explode in front of your people, you're sending them a very clear message: *Don't bring me bad news— I don't want to hear it.*

Once your people start to realize this, they act accordingly by keeping any bad news from you. But you can't make good decisions and proactively manage risks unless you have access to the most accurate and reliable information in near-real time.

A high-performance culture doesn't have any room for suppression of bad news. On the contrary, in a high-performance culture the rule of thumb is *bad news by rocket, good news by rickshaw*. People need to feel safe and supported to bring forward their views without fear of reprisal. What culture are you creating, if you're a landmine leader?

| The Teflon Leader

Another sign of low resilience is the leader who always finds a way to blame something or someone else when things go wrong. Nothing is ever their fault: any failure falls back on the customer, the regulator, the market, or a peer who didn't do what they were supposed to do. *Nothing* sticks to the Teflon leader. This is how they protect themselves from the fear that accompanies their low levels of resilience.

One of the core attributes of a resilient leader is the willingness to take accountability for what happens on their watch. They neither blame outside forces during times of adversity, nor do they give credit to those forces when they succeed. They know that everyone is dealt an equal share of good and bad luck, and they're confident in taking decisive action to try to shift the odds in their favor.

When you work for a Teflon leader, one thing stands out above all else: eventually *you* are going to be the one they blame in order to take the focus of underperformance away from themselves. This quickly drives a culture of conformance, avoidance, and dependence into even the most motivated team.

I worked with an executive many years ago whose ability to duck and weave to avoid accountability was near-genius level. Oliver was very bright, and would watch the organizational landscape incredibly closely to see where the likely successes and failures would arise. He had an uncanny knack for distancing himself from failures before they got too close to the crunch, even when those failures were clearly within his remit. But he also showed incredible skill at being able to swoop in at the 11th hour to claim credit for something he had little to do with.

The organization didn't benefit, nor did the people who worked in his group: even at the most senior levels, they were highly risk averse, lacked even the smallest modicum of creativity, and had neither the desire nor the ability to challenge this executive. It was the archetypal low-performing team.

The Catatonic Leader

The most common symptom of fragile leaders in stressful situations is that they freeze. They can't make decisions, and they're afraid to move in any direction, preferring to avoid the issue. *Maybe it will go away if I ignore it for long enough.*

This is not always obvious when looking from the outside in. The catatonic leader will often shroud their indecision in the noble cloak of thoughtfulness, deliberation, and prudence. But make no mistake: their fear of failure and lack of composure under pressure is pushing them deep inside themselves, and it can be just as damaging as the landmine leader's violent but quick reactions.

With a catatonic leader, the opportunity cost of delay destroys an organization's ability to respond effectively and to take control of a difficult situation. We saw a lot of this during the early days of the COVID-19 pandemic. Some of our political leaders were slow to react because, in all likelihood, they didn't want to be judged later for a poor initial response. Critical time was lost at a point when a delay of as little as a week could have widespread repercussions for a country or state.

I'm sure you already have a person's name in your head for each of these types of leaders who find it difficult to function under pressure. It's not hard to recognize these behaviors in other leaders, but we don't often recognize them in ourselves. This is our illusory superiority bias at work.

I once had to give some targeted feedback to one of my executives, Siva, after I heard him screaming at one of his leaders through a closed office door about 50 feet away. When I asked him why he was yelling, he looked at me innocently and said, "I wasn't." As I intensely studied his face, I realized that Siva genuinely believed this to be true. When I smiled, he demurred a little and added, "Well, I might have raised my voice just a bit."

This was the first time I'd observed anything remotely like this behavior from Siva, who had worked for me directly for almost two years. He may have been unaware of the intensity of his behavior, but he was at least aware enough to hide it from me. Sometimes, your people put as much energy (or more) into managing upward as they do getting the job done.

If you're serious about becoming a more resilient leader, it's good to have someone around you who's prepared to give you honest and consistent feedback about how you're projecting yourself, and how other people experience this. I learned an incredible amount over the years from the observations of trusted advisors who were courageous enough to tell me the truth, despite the risk it may have posed to them personally. For that, I'm grateful.

FOCUSING ON THE RIGHT THINGS

There are countless pithy, motivational quotes to convince us that we should welcome pain into our lives: *No pain, no gain... If we don't suffer the pain of discipline we suffer the pain of regret... What doesn't kill you makes you stronger... Pain is the feeling of weakness leaving the body.* Lots of people find this motivating. But, having just gone to some lengths to describe why willingly facing adversity is the only way to build resilience, I would also counter that by saying there's no nobility in needlessly struggling through pain that's easily avoided.

Let's begin to think about the tools, techniques, and mindset that will help you to better handle adversity, and to become more confident in your innate resilience. As your resilience develops, you'll find it much easier to be genuinely calm under pressure, and to remain in control regardless of the external circumstances.

The first tool is your ability to focus on the right things. Whenever there's a disruptive event or crisis, we tend to worry about the potential implications, as we seek to regain control of the situation. A really big part of handling any adversity is to work out what you can influence and what you can't.

You can burn an incredible amount of emotional energy on things that you have no control or influence over, and this limits your ability to deal with the things that you *can* influence. It distracts you from taking the action that might help to make a difference. Letting go of the things that are outside of your control is the first big step to handling adversity and becoming more confident in your own coping mechanisms.

Stephen Covey wrote the blueprint for this in his seminal work, *The 7 Habits of Highly Effective People*. He devised a model to help us separate the things we can control from the things we can't by using a visual model of two concentric circles—the *circle of influence*, which lies within the *circle of concern*.

There are many things in the world that are of concern or interest to us that we have no ability to change. They lie in the broad circle of concern. But there are many things we *do* have the ability to change, and these lie inside the smaller circle, the circle of influence.

Proactive people spend the majority of their time focusing on issues within their circle of influence, while reactive people spend their time focusing on issues within their circle of concern. You could also say that proactive people have an internal locus of control (*I shape my world by doing everything I can to influence it—what happens to me is largely the result of what I choose to do*) as opposed to an external locus of control (*Things always seem to happen to me that I have no control over—I'm a victim*).

The goal is to be proactive and focus your attention on your circle of influence. In fact, I like to take this model a step further and divide that circle of influence into two distinct components: the circle of influence and a smaller concentric circle within it, called the circle of control.

This helps us to make the further distinction between those things that are physically within our direct control, and those that we don't control but can influence. We'll see why this is important in dealing with adversity shortly. The adapted model looks like this:

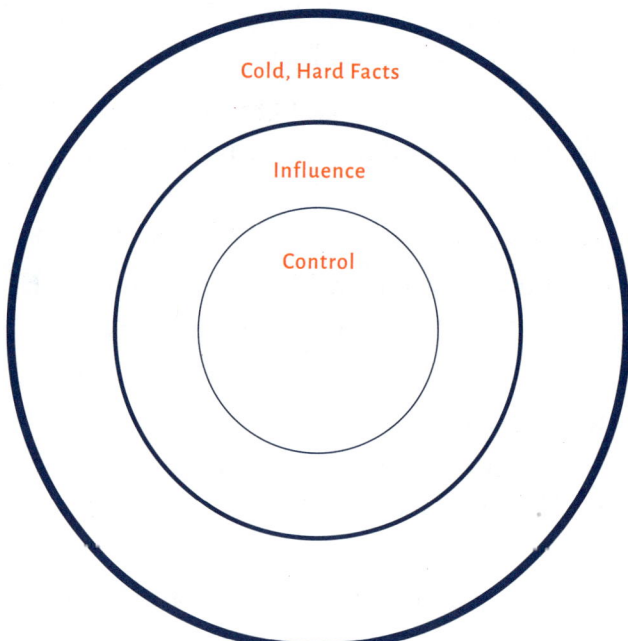

Figure 2: Classifying inputs to focus on the right things

I've called those things we can't change the *Cold Hard Facts*. We have total control of what lies in the innermost circle, and no control at all over what lies in the outermost circle. Let's have a quick fly over this model using an example.

In the summer of 2017, wholesale electricity prices rose dramatically in Australia. Prices had been relatively stable for a number of years, and probably artificially low as a result of oversupply in the market. However, with the introduction of excessive wind and solar generation power in several regions, two major coal-fired power stations were decommissioned. This radically changed the supply/demand balance in the market, and prices exploded.

After years of inferior performance, and with half a billion dollars of retained losses on the company balance sheet, we saw an opportunity to increase profits and to pay down a large portion of the company's debt. We devised our electricity trading strategy accordingly—not overly aggressive, but certainly capable of capturing some of this market value.

But life is never that simple. The steep increase in prices impacted our customers, particularly in the large industrial sector, to the point where it became a major issue for us with government, the energy market regulator, and the media. Some of our customers decided that the best way to attack the problem was to attack the players in the market to force government and regulatory intervention.

Inaccurate and hyperbolic stories began to appear in the media. A handful of electricity generation companies were accused of gaming the market to cause price spikes. This was patently untrue, but once the media fuse is lit, it can be hard to extinguish.

I had to lead the company so that our people didn't jump at shadows, become angry and distracted, or start to believe what they were reading in the daily paper.

| The Cold Hard Facts

Much of this situation was completely beyond our control, and the first thing we did was to understand the things that we couldn't change:

- Australia didn't have a cohesive energy and climate policy.

- Two large, critical power stations had been withdrawn from the market.

- Electricity prices had risen sharply.

- Customers, particularly heavy users of electricity, were hit hard financially.

- Some customers chose to run a campaign to force intervention in the market.

- Our company had been accused of profiteering.

- The media picked up on the business and political rhetoric to run the story.

- We could potentially suffer loss of profits, and long-term brand damage.

- This situation was unlikely to change any time soon.

We needed to understand these cold hard facts in order to formulate our response. But we spent no time complaining about them, agonizing over them, or wishing they were different. Once we understood what we were dealing with, we put the cold hard facts to the side and never revisited them, except to recalibrate as the environment shifted.

| Control

The next thing we did was to work out what we could control. There's actually very little that falls into this category, but it can be surprisingly powerful. Each of us controls a few basic things: What we *think*, what we *say,* what we *do,* and how we *behave.*

We first developed a situational risk analysis and messaging for our board of directors and shareholders. If we were to chart a way through this crisis, we needed their support. The board, with its many individual and collective obligations, needed to have accurate information to weigh when deciding how to respond.

We then chose the communication we would issue to our people, starting with the guidance I gave the executive team. We knew that the accusations were inaccurate—and we knew why—so I gave the direction to hold firm on our strategy.

Next, we had to formulate our media strategy. Responding to media allegations can be tricky, as some journalists just want a story that sells, while others are more interested in bringing balance and facts to their readers. But in a market as complex as the wholesale electricity market, it's awfully difficult to rise above the he said/she said glibness of any issue. We decided to do very few interviews, issued brief written denials to accusations where we thought appropriate, and let the rest of it go through to the catcher's mitt.

I undertook a tour of our operating facilities to explain to the people in each of our power stations what was happening, and why. If I hadn't done this, their only information feed would've been the morning media—the onsite leadership was focused on operational matters, as they should have been.

More than anything, I remained calm, optimistic, and rational. My executive team saw, as did anyone in my physical proximity, that I didn't see this as a big deal. We were doing everything we could to navigate the situation, I was confident in the team's ability to respond, and we would get through this with the best outcomes humanly possible.

| Influence

It's surprising how much influence we can have if we're committed to doing whatever we can to drive value for our stakeholders. We realized that there were many channels through which to exert our influence and make our efforts in our circle of control even more effective.

We sought to influence our myriad stakeholders with high-quality, frequent communication. We sought to influence the public discourse with a well-constructed media campaign. We found a way to apply commercial pressure to those customers who were spreading baseless rumors in the public domain, encouraging them to cool their jets. We sought to influence the inevitable witch hunts that continued even after the initial heat died down. And through my board position on the Australian Energy Council, the preeminent industry association, I sought to influence the country's policy settings.

Some of these influencing strategies were more effective than others—I'm certain I had absolutely no bearing at all on Australia's climate and energy policy—but that's not the point. The point is that I was paid, as CEO, to do everything within my power to drive value for the company, and those things were within my power.

The reason all of this is important in building your resilience is that it gives you the structure and technique to handle any adverse situation with composure, preserving your valuable energy for the things that can actually make a difference. In turn, this builds your confidence, because you know that you can handle any situation with relative ease and comfort.

Rather than trying to avoid or ignore adverse situations, you'll begin to relish the opportunity to put your leadership capability to the test by guiding your people through to the other side of any crisis.

As the great man himself, Stephen Covey, said, "I am not a product of my circumstances. I am a product of my decisions."

DEVELOPING PERSPECTIVE

Even when we become proficient with models like the circles of control, influence, and cold hard facts, our fear often gets the better of us. I see this constantly, even in good people who instinctively know what to do, but are overcome by the fear of failure. *What if I make the wrong decision, or do the wrong thing?*

It's precisely these thoughts that push people to become the catatonic leaders mentioned previously. That's why one of the best resilience tools we can have in the face of adversity is our ability to put any event into perspective.

This can be difficult, as we tend to be dominated by the here and now (and the recent past). Our brains try to protect us by training our focus on the danger at hand. This pushes us straight to the worst-case scenario.

What would happen if we made the worst-case scenario our friend?

More often than not, the answer to the question *What's the worst that can happen?* is much less frightening than we think. For the vast majority of us, we aren't landing space shuttles or performing cardiothoracic surgery. The stakes in our jobs just aren't that high—they're immaterial to our long-term success, happiness, and well-being.

Rather than panicking or agonizing over the worst-case scenario, what if you could learn to embrace it rationally, understand it for what it is, and then deal with it? One of the best things you can do to eliminate your fear is to understand the worst-case scenario, and then to ask a series of questions that demystify and disperse the cloud that envelopes you.

Start with the cold hard facts. Once something has happened, it's done. It can't be changed or bargained away, so why would you spend energy wishing it were different? Understanding it for what it is—its immediate and long-term impact on the organization and its stakeholders—sets the floor. Knowing where that floor is, and knowing that whatever actions you take from that point forward, will only improve the potential outcomes, energize you differently, and position you with a forward-looking focus.

Take Control

Most importantly, when you're a leader in the path of adversity, step clearly and confidently into your accountability to resolve the issue. If you're nervous, apprehensive, or fearful, this act alone will make you feel better.

The people around you will feel a sense of relief and confidence just knowing that you're owning the problem. It doesn't matter whether or not the problem was of your making, whether or not it was foreseeable, and whether or not you have a plan. Taking accountability immediately reduces the heat.

Ask the Right Questions

Developing perspective, for you and your people, comes down to control and influence: understanding the situation in all its ugliness, and then working out what you can do to change or improve it. A critically important part of this is knowing which questions to ask—not to solve the problem itself in the first instance, but just to put everything into perspective and keep your people relaxed and functioning.

There are dozens of questions that can serve to bring perspective to a difficult situation. They can be used in many different contexts, from receiving a poor piece of feedback from your boss, to managing a major public relations crisis.

I find that asking the following questions, of both yourself and your team, brings perspective to any situation pretty quickly:

Question 1: Now that the event is over, what's left that we should be concerned about?

This will focus you and your people on the imminent threats moving forward, pushing you into the circle of influence.

Question 2: How material is the impact on our customers?

Looking at any crisis from someone else's perspective shifts your thinking, and the customer is the best place to start: they're the lifeblood of your organization.

Question 3: What's the worst-case scenario from here, moving forward?

This will help you to understand the downside impacts rationally and calmly.

Question 4: How big a deal will this be in a week/month/year?

One of the most useful tools is to cast forward, looking at the bigger picture to assess relative importance. This takes the heat out of the immediate danger in almost any scenario.

Question 5: How material is the financial impact on our organization?

Thinking about the most tangible impacts first will force you to deal with facts, not fear and conjecture.

Question 6: Who's most impacted by this situation, and what does it mean to them?

An extension of the customer question, this question puts you in a better headspace, and ultimately helps to mitigate some of the larger risks that you might ignore if you just chose to wallow in self-pity.

Question 7: What lasting impact, if any, will this have on our people?

Questions like this teach us that very few of the things we worry about have any material or lasting impact on our people.

Question 8: What lasting impact, if any, will this have on our business?

Once again, surprisingly few major crises have a lasting impact. This is a great question to take you out of the weeds and get you focused on the bigger picture.

Question 9: Will this do any permanent damage to the organization's reputation and brand?

The answer to this question is almost always no.

Question 10: Will this do any permanent damage to my personal reputation and brand?

Again, the answer is almost always no.

Asking the right questions, of yourself and others, gives you a calm confidence that's contagious. If you're not overly concerned, your people will take their cue from you. People learn through modeling, and no area of leadership has a greater impact on others than your ability to function calmly under extreme pressure.

GRACE UNDER PRESSURE

When I was younger, before my knees and a love of good red wine convinced me to stop, I ran a few marathons—26.2 miles (and it's the last 0.2 that really hurts!). I was never a quick runner, but I posted a few fairly respectable 3-hour 15-minute results.

People unfamiliar with the sport often ask me if 3:15 is a good time, so here's how I put it into perspective. The fastest human on the planet, Eliud Kipchoge, holds the world record for the marathon at just over two hours (2:01:39). In 1994, Oprah Winfrey ran a marathon in Arlington, Virginia, in just under four and a half hours (4:29:15). So my time of 3:15 puts me smack bang in between the fastest marathon runner of all time, and... Oprah!

The point I want to make is that when you train for a marathon, you learn to listen to your body extraordinarily well: every slight muscle twinge, every moment of increasing fatigue or lactic acid buildup—you feel it all. The art of listening to your body is an incredibly valuable skill to have. It's completely transferrable to any context that tests your limits, as the big crises you face during your career surely will.

Self-awareness starts with understanding and reading the signals that your body sends you. Working out how to adapt and manage these signals seamlessly is the path to grace under pressure.

If you can feel yourself becoming angry or upset, you can deploy a coping strategy before that feeling takes hold of you. In the last chapter, we looked at the key to handling conflict in negotiations—your ability to feel any negative emotion, and immediately redirect it into curiosity.

We take this a little further when building resilience. The trigger (our immediate emotional response) is the same, but in a crisis we must drop quickly into taking accountability, focusing on the right things, and asking the questions that give us perspective. Sometimes, we'll try to do this and fail miserably—we simply don't read our emotions until it's too late. But with practice and discipline, you can get better at noticing your involuntary responses and redirecting them.

You can use any number of tools and techniques to help control your physical state. I've never been a big meditator, nor did I ride the wave of mindfulness that's become so popular in the last five years or so. But I've learned to incorporate breathing as a means of controlling my physical state. It can quickly move me from *fight or flight* mode into *rest and digest* mode. Everything is calmer, slower, and less confusing in that state.

Whatever you choose as your go-to technique, make sure you have something that you can deploy to manage your physical and emotional state. You'll need it.

Grace under pressure is incredibly valuable. It'll be noticed by your team, your peers, and the leaders above you. It has a lasting impact on culture. For example, if your people see you take bad news in stride, it'll be easier for them to come to you with issues. You'll get better information, faster. This fact alone will make you a better leader, and promote the constructive, high-performance culture that we'd all love to have in our teams.

Of all the leadership capabilities, resilience is the most accessible. It can be developed simply by facing the obstacles we find in our way, and getting safely to the other side. We don't have to go looking for roadblocks—life brings them to us naturally. We just need to learn to reflect, to listen, and to gain experience from the situations we find ourselves in.

Once we stop believing our own bullshit about how good we are under pressure, we're primed to use the few simple tools that will help to guide our reactions in any crisis. Work on the things you can influence—don't waste energy on anything else. Keep perspective, relax, and look forward with optimistic pragmatism to lead your team through even the most challenging events.

Calmness and composure are palpable and, before you know it, you'll find that you've developed a team of robust individuals who are equally cool in a crisis.

CUTTING THROUGH THE BULLSH!T

We're often seduced by our unconscious biases, which can dramatically affect our self-perception. It's easy to overestimate your level of resilience if you don't pay attention to how you respond under pressure. And you're also an excellent driver, right? That's why it's important to have someone around you who'll tell you the truth, whether you like it or not.

For each of the following questions, rate yourself (on a scale of 1 to 10) before you move on to the next chapter. This will give you greater insight into what stands between you and your ability to remain in control when the pressure is on.

1. How attuned are you to how others see you behave in adverse situations?

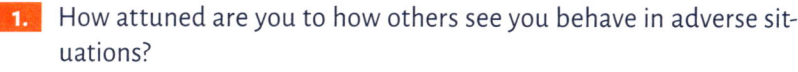

1   2   3   4   5   6   7   8   9   10

2. When you picture the three legs of your success stool (IQ, EQ, and AQ), how strong is the AQ leg?

1 2 3 4 5 6 7 8 9 10

3. To what extent do you rely on feedback to help understand your performance in tough situations?

1 2 3 4 5 6 7 8 9 10

4. To what extent did you relate to each type of nonresilient leader?

• Landmine leader

1 2 3 4 5 6 7 8 9 10

• Teflon leader

1 2 3 4 5 6 7 8 9 10

• Catatonic leader

1 2 3 4 5 6 7 8 9 10

5. How easy do you find it to separate issues into the things you can influence and the things you can't?

1 2 3 4 5 6 7 8 9 10

6. How easy do you find it to put any setbacks into longer-term perspective as soon as they occur?

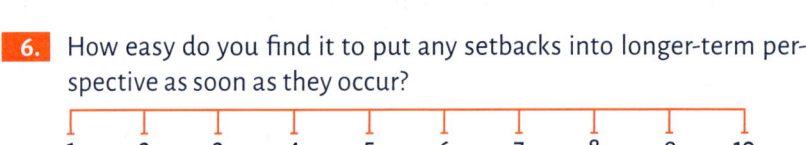

1 2 3 4 5 6 7 8 9 10

7. To what extent would your people say that you've acquired grace under pressure?

1 2 3 4 5 6 7 8 9 10

CHAPTER 5

WORK AT THE RIGHT LEVEL

THE BULLSH!T WE BELIEVE

We're told that it's important to lead by example—to not ask our team to do anything that we aren't prepared to do ourselves. It's sometimes called *leading from the front*, which sounds incredibly noble.

But this misguided philosophy can be dangerous. Many leaders use it as an excuse to bury themselves in the work of their people, to operate at a level of detail that's completely inappropriate for the level at which they're actually paid to work. Micromanagers who can't delegate control to their teams, or who aren't prepared to leave their comfort zone, will often justify these leadership flaws by saying "I'm leading from the front." Bullshit.

Leading from the front should be about setting high standards for performance and behavior—being an exemplar of unwavering commitment, strong work ethic, thoughtful ingenuity, and a focus on driving real results, not just going through the motions.

It should be about showing your people how to stretch by constantly stretching yourself—showing them how to be accountable by showing your own willingness to take accountability for outcomes. It should be about placing trust in people to do their jobs, and giving them clear feedback on how they've performed—not about doing their jobs for them.

Doing the work your people are paid to do is not leading by example, and it's not leading from the front. It's showing them that it's OK for you to get into their knitting, and it's telling them that they don't need to feel any real pressure to deliver, because they can happily cede control to those above them.

The truth is, you're paid to do a job, and the job at every level is different. Otherwise, why have levels at all? If you're busy doing someone else's job, you're not doing your own. Big problem! //

TWO KEY LEADERSHIP TRANSITIONS

There are two fundamental leadership transitions that we navigate as our careers evolve. When we're promoted through the hierarchy of an organization, or when our business grows beneath us, we have to accept that at each level we'll need different capabilities—the work fundamentally changes. Marshall Goldsmith first coined the phrase *what got you here won't get you there*, a great mantra to help you accept the inevitability of the transition.

Leader of Others

You start your working life as an individual contributor, concerned only with yourself. Your focus is on delivering your work on time, to a high standard. If you're particularly good at this, you'll also demonstrate some of the characteristics that the leaders above you look for in potential talent—initiative, creativity, the ability to communicate, a thirst for knowledge, and adaptability to changing work requirements and circumstances.

Your performance and behaviors may identify you as a high-potential employee, and you're earmarked for promotion into a leadership role. Once promoted, your role changes as you become a *leader of others*. It's a great feeling, that first promotion. It validates your performance, your intrinsic worth, and your potential for career advancement. But now, the very nature of the game has changed—you're now responsible for the output of a team of people, some of whom are less capable, less motivated, and less diligent than you are.

This is a great context in which to start learning the essential skills of leadership. *How can you get your people to adopt the same level of passion and drive that you bring to work each day?... How do you make sure the quality of everyone's work is acceptable?... How do you uncover any problems and issues while you still have time to remedy them?... And how do you deal with the people who are more interested in online shopping than doing the job they're paid to do?*

As a leader of others, you remain very close to the work that your team does. You have a direct reporting relationship with all of your team members, whom you can keep pretty close tabs on, for the most part. If you see any gaps, weaknesses, or problems emerge, it's very easy for you to step in and solve them yourself. We all do it when we start our leadership careers, and I was no different.

As a team leader running a small software development function for a bank, what I lacked in leadership experience and capability, I made up for in technical ability and work ethic.

I hadn't yet settled into this role when Alicia, one of the systems analysts, came to me with a tricky technical issue. After she'd explained the problem, I proceeded to outline the optimal solution, and sent her away to implement it exactly as I'd prescribed. The problem was resolved quickly, and the solution was rather elegant (even if I do say so myself).

I was very taken with my own brilliance, but what I failed to realize at the time was that I'd just missed a great opportunity to help Alicia to develop, and to lift her motivation and commitment. Instead, I'd taught her that if anything got too difficult, she could come to me and I'd fix it. I taught her that I was more than happy to do her job, if she ever didn't feel like doing it herself.

I'd also missed my own learning opportunity—to learn more about Alicia's capability and capacity. Rather than giving her the answer, if I'd asked some searching questions to help her arrive at a solution herself, we would have achieved the same outcome—but the difference would have been the development of Alicia's skills, knowledge, and judgment. This upside would have easily compensated for any extra time it may have taken to arrive at the outcome.

The environment you work in as a leader of others is usually very forgiving. If you do step in, no one is any the wiser, and it serves everyone's purposes—the job gets done, the team is stable, and you get to hone your technical skills, right?

Wrong. The temptation to step in and over-function for your people will be irresistible. But if this is your approach to problem solving, very soon you become a one-trick pony. Your people can't grow, because rather than giving them the opportunity to learn from their mistakes, you rescue them. You spend too much time with the poor performers, and too little with the high performers. And, most importantly, the standard you set for individual performance is low. As a result, the team can't function without you.

But when I look back now, my transition to a leader of others was relatively easy. It wasn't until I became a *leader of leaders* that I started to work out that my approach created some serious problems.

Leader of Leaders

The second career transition is the move from being a leader of others to being a *leader of leaders*. This comes after your promotion to a role where you have multiple layers of people on your team. You have leaders reporting directly to you, each of whom may have teams reporting directly to them.

Unlike a leader-of-others role, this one is incredibly difficult to manage if you haven't already built some leadership capability. You can't just step in when a problem occurs and fix it yourself, because you're further away from the work that's going on at the front line, and it's less visible. You have leaders in between you and those workers who also have an important role to fulfill. Your intervention hinders rather than helps their cause, and can quickly sour the relationships you have with the leaders below you.

As a leader of leaders, you have to let go of the details, spend less time concerned about the individual outputs of any one team, and focus on higher-order objectives. Although you may have been able to largely avoid this as a leader of others, you now have no choice but to start doing the work that leadership demands.

You can't waste time on details that you're paying other people to handle. That's their job, not yours. Your job is to set the objectives that align with the organization's strategy and tactical plans. It's to mobilize people and resources to meet those objectives, which *must* deliver tangible value.

You job is to make sure that you have the talent and capability in your team to deliver results, without you or your leaders having to continually step in. You need to lift your gaze to talent management and succession planning—

getting the right people on board to build a strong organization at every level.

You're now starting to see the shift in how you get results. Even at the leader-of-others level, you could get results through sheer will and brute force, leveraging your control. As a leader of leaders, results come through influence— a subtle but important shift in how you exercise power.

The expert power that's derived from your technical knowledge becomes less useful the higher up you go. The legitimate power that's attached to your position in the hierarchy can help you to get short-term results, but won't win the long-term commitment of your people. Your ability to wield coercive power to bend people to your will creates a culture of fear. Even the power that gives you the ability to grant or withhold rewards is only useful in a limited context. It's your referent power, the power of influence, that gets sustainable results and builds a constructive, high-performance culture.

They say that the true test of leadership is what people do when you're not there to watch them. This is the yardstick for a leader of leaders.

Most people who are promoted to a leadership role handle the first transition reasonably well. The team doesn't skip a beat, for all the reasons we've just discussed. The only real change is that the newly promoted leader of others picks up some additional workload, which seems like a fair exchange for the increased remuneration that comes with the new role. Everyone's happy.

But very few people handle the second transition well, and each promotion exacerbates the problem, making the holes in their leadership performance all the more obvious. Let's look at one example from my recent past.

Jason was a great worker in a mission-critical function of the business. He was diligent, thoughtful, communicated well with others, and had great attention to detail. In his specialist area, he delivered high-quality results. It wasn't long before these attributes caught the attention of his senior leaders, and he was promoted to a leadership role.

Even at this early stage, the cracks in Jason's leadership capability started to appear. When one of his people didn't deliver, he simply stepped in and did it for them. Occasionally, when something was beyond his reach, he would lower the standard that he demanded from his team—sometimes he'd let a deadline slip; other times he would drop a piece of work altogether, claiming that he didn't have sufficient resources to get it done. We've all done the same.

His team required specialist expertise from an external service provider. However, Jason had little commercial nous and didn't set up and manage the relationship competently. He was still buried in the detail of his team's work, rather than managing the supplier relationship. As a result, we ended up overpaying for something that wasn't clearly defined or governed.

When challenged on these issues, Jason always came back to the same excuse—"I don't have enough resources," which, like all excuses, sounds to me like "the dog ate my homework."

Instead of trying to work out how to leverage the expertise of the external supplier more prudently, he let them run the agenda. Instead of dealing with the underperformers in his team, he did more of their work himself. And when he ran out of bandwidth to do that, he hired more people—the wrong people—because he liked them, not because they were capable of doing the job.

Everything that could be done to create a poor-performing team, he did. Eventually, frustration and burnout got the better of Jason, and he moved to another organization—where, unfortunately, he'll likely repeat the same pattern.

BECOMING A PROFESSIONAL LEADER

When you ask children what they want to be when they grow up, they naturally imagine an occupation that involves *doing*, not *leading*. *I want to be an astronaut... I want to be a firefighter... I want to be a doctor so that I can cure all the diseases in the world...* I've never heard a child say "I want to be a professional leader."

We carry this story around in our heads from a very young age. Being a worthwhile person who can win the approval of our parents and teachers demands that we contribute in ways that are only available to individual contributors. What would give us a compelling reason to let go of this belief?

The first obstacle is the psychological and emotional impact that we experience as our professional identity shifts from being a specialist to a generalist, from an expert to a novice. We looked briefly at these impacts in Chapter 1. Letting go of expertise that defines us, that dictates our market value, and that has been a huge part of our personal story is never going to be easy.

Understanding the value of leadership is the key, and if you turn the final page of this book having learned nothing else, my wish for you is that you'll actually see leadership in a different light. Not only is leadership a worthwhile pursuit, but it can deliver many multiples of the value created by an individual, no matter how outstanding that individual might be.

So let's begin with the end in mind. Picture your ultimate career goal. Perhaps it's being the CEO of a major company, or perhaps it's growing your start-up venture into a multi-billion-dollar enterprise. Whatever the goal, there's a gap between where you are now, and where you'll be once that goal is realized.

Regardless of your original career choice, if your ambition is to lead a successful organization, you need to let go of childhood beliefs about what creates your intrinsic worth. You need to become a professional leader.

As an individual contributor, your focus is a mile deep and an inch wide. Your value comes from your knowledge, expertise, and capability in a narrow field of endeavor. But fast-forward to your final career destination, and your focus is a mile wide and an inch deep—quite the opposite.

Somewhere between here and there, a shift has to occur. A shift in thinking, a shift in behavior, and a shift in capability. Let's look at the dynamics of how this works.

| The First Transition

Figure 3 shows your state as an individual contributor. The orange box demonstrates your narrow field of vision as an accountant. You're there to do accounting work, nothing else.

The time clock is important here—the area of the rectangle represents the amount of time you spend working on the job.

It's important to realize that this is context-dependent. For example, if you're working as an accountant in a government agency, the area of the rectangle might represent a commitment of 37.5 hours per week. However, if you're working as an accountant in one of the large consulting firms, it may represent a commitment of 70 hours per week or more. Whatever the number, it's a finite amount of time based on the cultural expectations of your organization, and your individual willingness to meet those expectations.

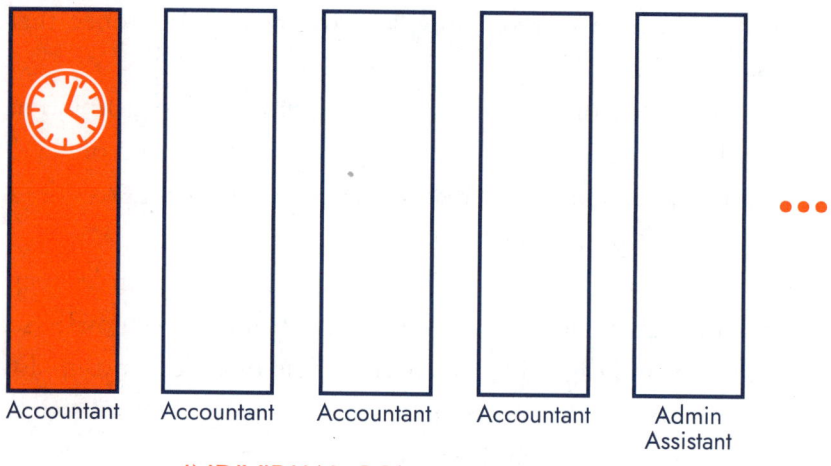

Accountant Accountant Accountant Accountant Admin
Assistant

INDIVIDUAL CONTRIBUTORS

Figure 3: Work and time allocation for an individual contributor

When you transition to a leader-of-others role, you adopt a broader perspective and outlook in order to manage the overall outputs of the team.

Two important things change. The first is the horizon you look toward. Individual contributors can look day to day, week to week, month to month. As a team leader, you have to look farther ahead. *Are we on track to meet our targets for this year?... How do I shift my resources to handle the end of the fiscal year?... What do I need to do to support the external auditors, and whom should I assign to work with them?*

The second important change is that the area of your new rectangle becomes larger. You have more work to get through, and often the only way to do that is to work longer hours. That is, of course, until you realize what your job truly is, and learn how to do it in a way that utilizes your personal capacity most effectively.

Figure 4 demonstrates this shift. If you're spending too much time doing the work of your people instead of working out how to stretch them to deliver better-quality work more efficiently, the area of the rectangle increases, which at some point diminishes your ability to work effectively. You need to be close to the action, but you clearly can't do everything yourself.

Building capability in your team enables the predictable delivery of high-quality results. This takes a lot of energy and commitment up front, but once it's done, it's done. From that point on, you can spend less time focusing *in and down*, and more time focusing *up and out*.

Here's the great truth of this transition: you'll be given choices. You can choose to increase your time and effort by 10 percent, or maybe even as much as 20 percent. But what impact will that have compared to the potential impact of getting 10 percent more out of every individual on your team? Focusing on your leadership, even at this early stage of your career, can produce results that other teams can't match—purely because you worked out how to put your time and energy into the *right* things.

Figure 4: Work and time allocation for a team leader

| Reaching Your Ultimate Goal

The transition to a leader–of–leaders role will challenge you even more, because you won't have visibility into all the work your teams are doing. You ultimately can't control everything everyone does, and if you spend too much time trying to, the negative impact on your people is incredible. We'll talk about the detrimental impacts of a micromanager shortly, but let's just stick to our focus on time management.

As you progress to higher levels of an organization's hierarchy, your focus has to shift to competently cover a much greater scope of accountabilities. *Figure 5* shows what this looks like for the chief executive of a major business. With multiple heads of department and operating divisions, you have to work out how to get across the substance of every division, without being able to smell, touch, and taste it. You have to rely on your senior executives to do their jobs, to look after their own portfolios.

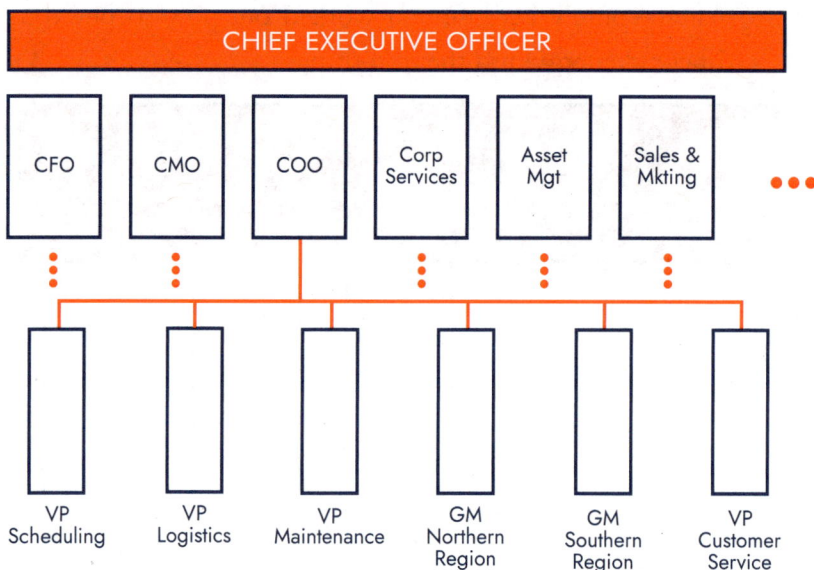

Figure 5: Work and time allocation for a chief executive

You'll find that you spend an increasing amount of your time guiding and leading them, not trying to work out what's happening in the accounting team where you started. How interesting that an accountant needs to become competent in marketing, operations, public relations, contract law, and asset management!

Can you imagine the commitment of time and effort that would be required on the CEO's part if they weren't able to trust and lead their executives to achieve the necessary outcomes? This is the paradox of increasing accountability with decreasing control that you will inevitably face, if you haven't already. The CEO role isn't even remotely doable unless you master the art of staying above the detail, and building the talent and capability to get that extra 10 percent out of every individual.

The earlier you learn to leave your technical expertise behind and lead, the smoother your transition will be from your childhood career aspiration to your ultimate goal.

LEAVE A LEVEL, LEAVE A COMFORT ZONE

In order to adapt to any new level, you have to accept an inalienable truth: that you'll feel pretty uncomfortable when you first move to that level. And if you don't feel uncomfortable, you're not doing it right. Feeling comfortable is a sign that you've not faced the transition head-on—it's more likely that you're spending your time doing many of the same things you did before your promotion. It feels good to be immersed in familiar pursuits.

But one of the basic tenets of organizational design is that every layer of the structure must have a unique purpose. If not, it shouldn't exist—it's just an unnecessary cost overhead.

Working out what to do in a new role isn't as easy as it should be, for a number of reasons. First of all, when you're hired into a new role, it's expected that you'll automatically know what to do. Some of this is your own fault—remember, you just spent time and effort convincing the person who hired you that you *already* know what to do. Secondly, your boss has a number of pressing priorities that are always going to outweigh their desire and ability to spend time holding your hand and making sure your transition is a success.

It shouldn't be that way, but it typically is.

The first place to look is your team, and at the talent and capability that exists both individually and collectively. If this doesn't raise some discomfort, then something's wrong. Most teams have gaps in capability, performance, and culture. If you don't see them initially, look again. Teams have a habit of carrying people because of their longevity, their relationships, or sometimes simply through the lack of will on the part of previous leaders to set a high performance bar.

Taking stock of your talent, without any preconceived notions of what you might find, will give you something to think about and work on for the first several months in your role, even if you were to do nothing else. Increasing the depth of your gene pool is difficult and time-consuming, but it has one of the biggest paybacks of any leadership activity.

Discovering what it means to work at the right level comes by working through a series of questions.

Question 1: What's the primary objective of my new role?

Promotion to any new role should give you pause to consider why your new role exists. If you go back to your tools from Chapter 2 and look at the job through the lens of value creation, the purpose of the role will soon become apparent.

For example, moving from being a floor supervisor in a factory to being the manager of the same facility requires a significant shift in focus. As a supervisor, your main concern was the productivity and safety of people and machines. But as the manager, you'll need to let someone else work out those individual details while you concentrate on higher-order considerations, such as overall plant capacity, the production targets set by corporate, customer demand, process controls, and product quality. It's a completely different role, focusing on a completely different time horizon.

Question 2: How does this differ from my previous role?

Even though you may have confidently answered the first question, this question helps you to explicitly understand the tasks that you need to leave behind. The adage of getting rid of the old to make way for the new applies perfectly here. This is how you make conscious choices about no longer carrying out the activities of your old role, which would see you working at the wrong level. The more explicit you can make this process, the more likely you are to not slip back into old habits.

Question 3: In what way is this role broader than my last role?

Most promotions have the effect of giving you a broader scope of responsibilities. You become accountable for things that you previously didn't have to concern yourself with. If we look at our previous example, even though a production supervisor in a factory mightn't need to know much about financial performance, a factory manager does.

Instead of just having operational workers reporting to you, you may now have to lead a financial controller, a human resources manager, and a procurement specialist.

That's on top of your need to lead the production supervisors, the role from which you've just emerged. This leads naturally to our next question.

Question 4: What capabilities do I need to acquire?

This question comes in two parts. The first is to assess the capability you have in the team, based upon the outcomes you need to achieve. For everything in your scope, you need to ensure that your team has the right capability (both quality and quantity). Do you have the right people to deliver results? If not, how do you build (or buy) this capability?

The second part is to assess your own capabilities, and to understand what you lack, if anything. How much do you need to know personally in order to lead the function competently, without undertaking the work yourself?

Question 5: What capabilities do I already have that are transferrable and valuable?

You almost always possess capabilities that will be highly valuable in your new role, despite the fact that your daily activities and focus may change significantly. For example, the skill you've developed in removing production bottlenecks as a factory supervisor can be built upon and adapted for capacity planning tasks. Your affinity with the workers you used to supervise can be called upon to gain their support and commitment for any changes you need to implement. Your detailed understanding of the unit costs in the part of the operation you used to run can be extended to create an activity-based costing model for the whole factory.

Work out how your existing capabilities can be refined for use at a higher level.

It's also useful to look to the more general elements of your skill set. A complete inventory of your capabilities in areas like communication, negotiation, financial literacy, influencing, and relationship building will give you the confidence to take on any new role.

Question 6: What does my new boss expect?

We often try to infer what our boss wants, without explicitly seeking a conversation with her about it. Perhaps you can glean some of it from your list of annual KPIs, or your formal position description. But unless you make a deliberate effort to ask your boss what she needs from you, and what her expectations are, she's unlikely to give you the clarity required to do your job properly.

I've seen an incredible number of mismatches between the expectations of a boss and the understanding of those expectations by a leader who's trying to meet them. It's mind-boggling to think that this disconnect exists, even though a simple conversation could help a new leader understand and calibrate these expectations.

Question 7: What new relationships are important to me?

A new level reveals a whole new peer group for you to deal with. In modern organizations, very little is achieved within a single portfolio. Cooperation, collaboration, and communication are staples in any senior leader's repertoire.

Understanding which groups are essential in enabling you to deliver high-value outcomes for your organization will help you to determine which relationships are most critical to your (and your team's) success. Explicitly nurturing these relationships opens the door to execution excellence.

You will also need to develop external relationships with, for example, suppliers, customers, regulators, stock analysts, and community groups. Building strong external relationships can be the difference between success and failure.

Question 8: What new groups have I become part of?

As with your new relationships, many promotions result in you joining new groups. For example, as factory manager you may be invited to join two new groups—the company's operations leadership team and the central safety committee. Each requires some thought if you're going to contribute to these forums effectively.

I was always at pains to remind the executives who worked for me that they had two distinct but important roles—one as the head of the portfolio that they were responsible for (operations, finance, strategy, etc.), and a second as a member of the company's executive team. The latter required effort and energy beyond simply delivering results from the teams under their direct control.

The executive accountable for the company's operations didn't have the luxury of focusing solely on operations—he didn't get a free kick on his obligation to understand and contribute to the company's broader financial performance at the executive level.

Question 9: What symbols of transition do I need to put in place?

If your promotion is within the same organization, and especially if it's stepping into your boss's former role, it's important to change people's perceptions of who you are and what you do. Once you've worked your way through this series of questions, it's important to communicate your new approach and focus to those around you.

Explicit conversations with key stakeholders will yield the best results. They don't have to be lengthy conversations, but they do have to be deliberate. A conversation with a peer could go something like this: "Mike, I've thought a lot about my new role. Here are the things I'm going to focus on, and here are the things that I'll no longer be doing. I'd really appreciate your support to help me get my feet under the desk quickly."

Discomfort is an unavoidable part of any new role, until you become familiar with it. If you can quickly gain a good understanding of what you need to do differently, that discomfort will be short-lived. It's the platform upon which you build a new comfort level with a completely different set of parameters for your performance, and ultimate success.

DON'T DIP DOWN

We *dip down* when we do the work of the people below us in the organizational hierarchy. It's not what we're paid to do, and there's rarely a justifiable reason for doing it, no matter how much we try to rationalize why it's necessary. As Jeffrey J. Fox says, "Don't hire a dog and bark yourself."

Dipping down is destructive for you, for your people, and for the culture of your team. The dynamics are easy enough to explain, but often difficult to see in the heat of the moment, as we tend to react instinctively without thinking through the consequences of what we're doing. Like most problems we face, awareness is the first step to change.

| The Impact on You

Dipping down perpetuates your bad habits and creates a barrier to your growth as a leader. It reinforces your need for control and your ability to quickly resolve any problem simply by applying more personal effort to it.

Instead of working with your people to lead them to a higher standard of performance, you allow them to use you as a crutch. This plays into your primal need for security by reinforcing that you're truly indispensable.

Most of all, dipping down ensures that you're constantly busy—too busy to do the work of leadership, which you may be subconsciously avoiding. Having difficult conversations, setting high standards for performance and behavior, understanding and communicating the objectives of your team, and challenging every piece of activity that's going on to ensure it delivers maximum value—that's the work of leadership.

When you reach a sufficiently high level, dipping down creates two problems—first, your workload becomes increasingly oppressive, and second, your interventions become proportionally less effective. You only have so many fingers to plug the holes in the dike, and in the absence of strong talent and capability in your team (which it's your job to build) you'll find yourself uncomfortably exposed by your team's weaknesses.

| The Impact on Your People

When you dip down, you're sending a very clear message to your people: *I don't trust you to do your job. I have to get in there and help you to do your job, or do it for you.* This sucks the motivation out of your people faster than you can say "Great work, team!" No amount of rhetoric speaks as loudly as your actions when you dip down. People instantly become disempowered, disinterested, and disengaged.

If you consistently demonstrate that this is how you operate, an interesting dynamic develops. People stop giving you their best efforts. They know that if something isn't delivered to the required standard, you'll step in and fix it for them. They learn not to be innovative, believing that anything they do will eventually be overturned by you anyway. They become passive and subservient, unproductive and bored.

Working for someone who continually dips down has a debilitating effect that no amount of rationalization about leading from the front can quell. Just as dipping down demonstrates a lack of trust in your people, they learn not to trust you either. The prerequisite for a healthy leader-follower relationship is destroyed.

The Impact on the Culture

When you get involved in other people's work in a detailed manner, the accountability that they *should* hold for delivering the outcomes they've been assigned is diluted. You effectively begin to share this accountability with them, because you've usurped their autonomy, choice, and empowerment. This is the thin edge of the wedge in the breakdown of an effective execution culture.

As we discovered in Chapter 2, a philosophy of excellence over perfection is essential to fostering a healthy, value-driven culture. If you truly want a culture where people are prepared to have a go, to experiment within safe boundaries, and to give their discretionary effort to the job, don't dip down.

A culture where a leader micromanages every detail quickly becomes stodgy and conformist, as it's solely dependent on the leader to make every decision and approve every action. Even without considering all the other impacts, these bottlenecks alone are sufficient reason for you to avoid dipping down.

Dipping Down vs. Inspecting Progress

Inspecting progress is an essential part of a leader's role in driving successful execution of work, and should be guided by Ronald Reagan's simple adage: "Trust, but verify."

I've often been asked what the difference is between dipping down and inspecting progress. There are two main distinctions. The first is the level of detail interrogated. Having regular checkpoints to satisfy yourself that a particular piece of work is on track, and that the accountable person is progressing as expected, is essential—as long as it doesn't become an inquisition into every minute detail, decision, and nuance of their work.

The second difference is how you articulate the enquiry. When things go off track, as they inevitably will, the role of the leader is to ask good questions focused on the agreed outcomes to understand why a problem has occurred, and what needs to be done to get it back on track. Questions like:

• Was this issue foreseeable?

• When did you first get the sense that there might be a problem?

• Do you feel as though you fully understand the root cause of the problem?

• Do you have everything you need to resolve the issue yourself?

• If not, what do you need from me now?

• Who else does this problem affect—are there any dependencies?

• How should I adjust my expectations on this deliverable?

• Now that we know about this issue, is there anything else you're working on that might face similar problems?

Asking the right questions is very different from arriving at the scene of a disaster with a red cape around your shoulders and your underwear on the outside, and proceeding to fix the problem yourself.

People have to gain experience somehow. As a general principle, you should let people succeed or fail on their own merits and learn from their mistakes. But this is not to say that you should *never* intervene in the detailed work of your people.

Dipping down may occasionally be necessary to avoid an imminent disaster. The principle of letting your people fail only goes so far, and it would be negligent to stand back and watch a catastrophe unfold.

A good analogy is standing at the side of a busy road with a toddler, let's call him Johnny, waiting to cross. If Johnny tries to break free from your grip and run into traffic, what do you do? This is *not* the time to let Johnny make his own decision and test his boundaries. This is *not* the time to turn to Johnny and calmly explain the pros and cons of running onto a busy road. This is *not* the time for indulging Johnny with a Socratic line of questioning to awaken his consciousness to the risks posed by moving automobiles.

This is the time to yell at Johnny with all the urgency you can muster, and grab him by any body part you can reach to wrench him back from the path of oncoming traffic.

I once made the decision to step into the middle of an outsourcing decision that my negotiating team was poised to sign. I didn't believe that the chosen supplier's risk profile was adequate for a long-term arrangement to provide a critical service. So I overruled them and sent them back to the drawing board. Would the agreement have ended in catastrophe? Maybe not, but if I didn't believe that it was a very strong possibility, I wouldn't have stepped in.

Occasionally, intervening to override the natural instincts of your people may be warranted. But before doing so, always ask yourself the question *Am I watching a critical failure unfold where the consequences might be catastrophic, or I am just dipping down because that's how I roll?*

DEALING WITH A MICROMANAGING BOSS

Even if you're at the top of the food chain, you always answer to someone, and that someone might be a micromanager who only feels comfortable when they're dipping down into your work. This can be demoralizing if you don't get on top of it quickly.

You need to accept the fact that you're not going to fundamentally change someone at a senior level who hasn't chosen to make the transition to leadership. They'll continue to rely upon their intellect, experience, and position in the organizational hierarchy to achieve results. But you do need to establish agreed boundaries for your relationship that will enable you to dampen the negative effects of a micromanager.

The first rule is to explicitly communicate the impact of the interference from above. When a leader dips down, most people below them don't attempt to establish any sensible boundaries. Instead of confronting the issue and risking a potential conflict with the boss, people tend to go along with it, opting for subservience. But bitching and moaning about your boss around the watercooler (or over Zoom) won't change the reality of your situation.

Even though you may not be able to fundamentally change your boss's approach, you have more power than you realize in setting the tone for how they work with you. Over the years, I've discovered some useful statements and questions to help me establish the right working relationship with the leaders I was working for. If you have a decent relationship with your boss, these can be very powerful. Try pushing back with a few simple statements:

- You need to trust me with this.

- I understand the objectives I've agreed to, and I'm confident I'll deliver on those.

- The project is on track; you don't need to worry about anything at this stage.

- I'll let you know if anything changes, but everything is in good shape at the moment.

There are dozens of variations on this theme, but the principle is to let your boss know that you have confidence in your ability to deliver. You can easily show that everything is on track because, naturally, you're managing the process well, and any interference from your boss is exactly that—interference.

You may have to go further if the conversations you're having don't seem to be taking root. The next level is to ask questions of your boss that explore the reasons behind their unwanted interventions:

- What would give you confidence that I'm on top of this work?

- Is there anything that you need to see from me that you're not seeing at the moment?

- What do you need me to do that I'm not currently doing?

Once again, there are many questions that can be used here to encourage your boss to voice his discomfort. More often than not, the answer is, "Oh, no, I don't want you to think there's something wrong. I trust you, I just wanted to check on a few things." You don't have to have too many of these conversations before your boss backs off and leaves you to manage your own accountabilities.

On the odd occasion that they do have an issue, you've cleverly invited your boss to tell you what that issue is. Although not every boss will respond to your cue (and if they do, you might not like what you hear), it does give you clarity and transparency on what's driving their behavior. Then at least you have something you can work with.

Many years ago, I worked for a gentleman who was, by most measures, a great boss. Doug had an incredible intellect, unimpeachable ethics, and an impeccable set of values. To top it off, he didn't have a bone of self-interest in his body. Doug had an insatiable appetite for complex information, and could comfortably get across the detail at every level between him and the front line of the project team.

But there were occasions when I had to subtly push back, as Doug liked to engage in content way below his pay grade. In one of our one-on-one meetings, he asked a few questions about some of the details in a particular area of the project, which was three levels below me. My response? I simply asked, "Doug, why would I know that?"

The penny dropped for him immediately. Those six simple words made him realize that we were paying other people to do that work and if I wasn't interested in the nitty-gritty details, then my boss probably shouldn't be either.

That was the last time we needed to have the conversation, and we enjoyed a strong working relationship for many more years.

MAKING YOURSELF PROMOTABLE

If you have a shred of ambition, you most likely want to be noticed, and to be promoted to higher roles within your organization. If you run your own business, you want to be able to grow without hitting the founder's ceiling that sees many ceding control to an external management team to take the company forward through its next phase of growth.

Whatever your situation (even if you're comfortable remaining in the role you currently occupy) you want to stand out as being *first amongst equals*. Working at the right level has a big influence on how you're perceived by those around you, and you want to create the right perceptions.

If you create a strong dependency on yourself in the detailed functioning of your team, this eventually makes you indispensable *to that team*. No one will consider you for a promotion or new project if you can't create the space for that to happen. There's also a danger of becoming typecast as "the accounting guy," or "the marketing girl."

Don't get me wrong, you have to do your job and get results with the team you have, otherwise you have no foundation to build upon. There's no potential without performance, so the first step is to demonstrate that you can perform.

Rather than trying to make yourself indispensable, your first instinct should be to make yourself *redundant* at the earliest opportunity. Building team capability and performance that's largely independent of your efforts is the most responsible thing to do as a leader. That way, on the off-chance that you're hit by a bus (or a coronavirus), your team and organization won't suffer too badly—things can go on without major disruption.

In his book *Screw It, Let's Do It*, Richard Branson talks about the value of being able to rely on a highly capable team. "People have asked me how I can take so much time off to go on adventures around the world. My answer is that when you pick the right people, you can leave them to it. You know that things will run smoothly when you're not there."

Building strong capability and a track record of performance in your team will give you sufficient credibility without irrevocably tying you to every output the team produces. The first step to being promotable is to show that you have the ability to predictably achieve results through others, without the stress, chaos, and inward focus demonstrated by many who work at the wrong level.

| Dress for the Job You Want, Not the Job You've Got

This old adage isn't meant to be taken literally, of course. How you choose to dress has little bearing on your behavior and performance.

This is about lifting yourself above the noise, and thinking ahead to your next role. When anyone makes a decision about offering a promotion, they weigh up a number of risks. To mitigate those risks, they look for a demonstrated ability to operate at that level.

External candidates for a role can reduce the perceived risk, because they often already have experience at the level in question. The downside with external appointments is that you never know until you work closely with someone what they're *really* like. But they often look shiny in the interview room and, at senior levels, everyone has learned to talk a good game.

If you're going to convince anyone that promoting you to a new level isn't a huge risk, you need to demonstrate the qualities of someone already at that level. You need to *think* at that level…to handle the *complexity* at that level…to *communicate* at that level…to build *relationships* at that level. You want the decision makers to think *Wow! Hayley's really impressive. We have to find a way to get her up to the next level before someone else offers her a job and she leaves.*

Read, listen, and understand what that looks like for your next role, so that whenever you open your mouth, it's clear to everyone around you that you've already made the transition *inside yourself,* before you get the job to match.

One of my early executive roles was running a shared services division in a large rail transportation company. The division had around 1,000 people, and annual operating costs amounting to hundreds of millions of dollars (and these bloated numbers hid some massive inefficiencies).

The first time I met the CEO was in an executive meeting where I had to present a paper on how we planned to transform the procurement function, part of my shared services portfolio, into something commercially competitive. When a line of questioning emerged around the treatment of spare parts (and these were expensive parts), I engaged the CEO in a quick sidebar about the balance sheet impacts of decreasing our inventory turns and the implications for the financial ratios that drove the business.

Needless to say, that wasn't the norm for a shared services head, who would be more likely to spend their time buried in the minutiae of processes, service agreements, and supplier contracts. I demonstrated my ability to think and interact above the level at which I was being paid, and it wasn't too long before I was promoted.

| Be a Trusted Advisor, Not a Workhorse

Organizations are full of good soldiers—people who can be relied upon to get things done. Through this, they demonstrate their performance, not their potential. To be promotable, you have to show both. Everyone loves a good workhorse, but trusted advisors are few and far between.

The capability and willingness to challenge your boss and to have conversations with them at their level, so that you can add value to their thought processes and decisions, is rare. For the most part, this is greatly respected and appreciated, although you'll no doubt run into the odd boss who finds this threatening, stirring their darkest insecurities. Stay away from them!

Becoming a trusted advisor enables you to rapidly build credibility, respect, and connection, all of which count when you need your boss to support you in the broader organization. This becomes part of your personal brand—the thing you're known for.

You want to develop a personal brand that screams *You need to promote me now!* This comes through your role as a trusted advisor, with the emphasis on the word *trusted*. Like Robert Duvall's character in *The Godfather*, the advice from you has to be consiglieri-like—clear, well-intentioned, dispassionate, and coming from a place of impartiality, not self-interest.

Working at the right level is the key to confidently taking on any new role. So work feverishly to build a highly capable team that can deliver results, with or without you. Think carefully about what you should be doing (and why), and how your efforts can best drive value. If you don't, your wake-up call may come too late—at the end of a career for which you've traded off too much of your life. Family, health, and happiness are frequent casualties when you insist on working below your level. This would be a real shame, when all it would have taken is a better understanding of how to excel at leadership, without letting your career consume your life.

CUTTING THROUGH THE BULLSH!T

Establishing yourself at the right level for your role is important for so many reasons. As long as you're doing your people's work for them, they won't perform at their best, and you'll be too busy to do the job you're paid to do. But it's much more comfortable to hold onto the work that you're familiar with. Most leaders work below their level occasionally, but this should be the exception, not the rule.

For each of the following questions, rate yourself (on a scale of 1 to 10) before you move on to the next chapter. This will give you greater insight into what stands between you and your ability to confidently deliver results as you're promoted to higher levels in your organization.

1. How necessary do you feel it is for you to be involved in the detailed work of your team?

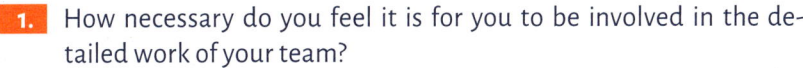

2. When you dip down, to what extent is it forced by

- lack of capability in the team below you?

- your need to control the outcomes?

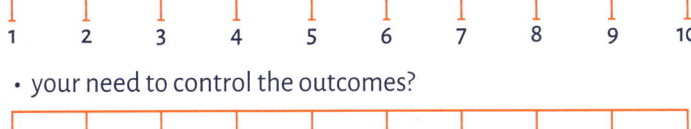

- the natural pull you feel toward technical work, rather than leadership work?

- a desire to retain your technical skills and perceived market value?

3. To what extent do you see opportunities to reduce your workload by working at the right level?

1   2   3   4   5   6   7   8   9   10

4. How easy did you find your transition to a new level when you were last promoted?

1   2   3   4   5   6   7   8   9   10

5. To what extent do you seek to achieve outcomes through other people, rather than yourself?

1   2   3   4   5   6   7   8   9   10

CHAPTER 6

MASTER AMBIGUITY

THE BULLSH!T WE BELIEVE

How many times recently have you heard a CEO or business owner say they've had to "pivot"? This normalizes random, knee-jerk responses to external shifts. It almost makes it seem like an organization that's failed in some respect is actually being well managed. Bullshit.

Agility is an important capability for any organization in the world of global commerce, but if we only focus our attention on dealing with events as they unfold, it's often too late to respond effectively. Whatever happened to anticipating the shifts in the market and environment, and moving decisively to set the pace for our competitors?

There's nothing wrong with the concept of changing tack when events demand it. But the complacency that creeps in when you don't manage the ambiguity in your environment *proactively* is dangerous. Mitigating a risk judiciously and deliberately in advance of a crisis is completely different to playing catch-up when you're forced by circumstances beyond your control to shift. And one day, you'll run out of luck.

As leaders, our job is to explore, absorb, and make sense of a highly ambiguous environment, not to throw our hands up in the air because we can't get the certainty we'd like. Our job is to sit comfortably in ambiguity, and translate it into clarity and certainty for our people. Individual contributors aren't paid to resolve ambiguity. But leaders are.

As you progress through the higher levels of any organization, ambiguity increases, complexity increases, and any answers you might have thought you had become less certain. What used to be a binary, black-and-white world morphs into a thousand shades of grey.

If you believe the bullshit that it's enough to simply pivot when something changes, you'll eventually run out of responses, while the gap between you and your competitors widens. You may even experience your own Kodak moment at some point in the future, when your company is completely left behind. //

THE JOB OF A LEADER

The acronym VUCA was coined in the late 1980s to describe a world that was becoming increasingly difficult to navigate—volatile, uncertain, complex, and ambiguous.

At the highest levels of a modern organization, you'll deal with a scope of work that will challenge your capacity. You'll also deal with a level of complexity that will test your abstract reasoning capability. You need to be able to sift through the mountains of available information, and synthesize it into useful insights. The value of the decisions you make balloons, as does the impact that these decisions have on your organization and its stakeholders. In short, everything you do is amplified.

The amount of ambiguity that you'll face in dealing with these challenges can be extremely unsettling, but in senior roles, it comes with the territory—that's why you get paid the dizzy dollars. But while you need to be capable of operating comfortably in extreme ambiguity, the people on the front line doing the day-to-day work that drives your organization don't.

Drawing a line from the top of the organization to the bottom, and being able to explain how the activity at every level is connected, is a core leadership imperative. It starts at the top with the purpose, vision, and values of the organization. This is formalized in the strategic plan, which paints the broad parameters for how the organization will compete in its market(s). The strategic plan provides high-level guidance, but it doesn't resolve ambiguity—after all, a strategy is just a set of principles around which to improvise.

From the strategy, the next layer of detail is captured in the organization's tactical planning. What are you going to focus on in the next two to three years to deliver on your long-term strategic goals? Which new assets should you look to potentially acquire? Which of your existing assets should you seek to divest? How do you reduce your cost base to be more competitive?

Tactical plans are further broken down into annual operating plans, which describe all of the activities that you're going to undertake this year to deliver the value defined by the higher-level objectives.

And at the front line, your people need to know what's expected of them *today*. What do they need to do to deliver the greatest value possible—what does "good" look like? How can they play their part in delivering the higher-order objectives that make the organization competitive, profitable, and sustainable?

Narrowing down uncertainty by defining the actions your people need to take—resolving ambiguity at each layer of the organization—is the job of leadership. Enabling your people to see how their work connects to the organization's highest-order objectives is one of the keys to successful execution.

Communicating this to your organization requires effort and intent. We'll deal with this later in this chapter, but at this point it's important to recognize that, without a compelling story, productivity will decline. In the absence of clarity, people spend a lot of time speculating about what may or may not be happening. This creates a feeling of helplessness that eats its way into your culture like a cancer.

Your job as a leader is to master ambiguity, and turn it into certainty for your people.

THE DARK SIDE OF AMBIGUITY

The inability to competently manage ambiguity manifests in a number of ways, but it's most commonly seen in one devastating symptom: lack of action. Leaders who can't construct clear answers, actions, and direction will often stall. They wait and see...they look for a sign...they do everything except take decisive action.

In the next chapter, we'll explore decision-making in some depth. One of the most critical elements of making great decisions is timeliness—speed over accuracy, every time. But for now, we'll focus on the implications of being unable to move forward and create a path for your people when ambiguity gets the better of you.

Regaining control of the narrative at times when uncertainty is at its greatest is key to leading your people well, and keeping them focused and productive. Without this, your lack of action becomes debilitating for those who rely on you. Here are a few ways this can affect your people and the broader culture:

| Trust Is Damaged

Your inaction inevitably leads to a lack of communication, and in the absence of clear communication, your people will feel exposed and vulnerable. Often, despite your best intentions, people read this as a lack of trustworthiness— *What isn't Vicki telling us?* Over time, this has a negative effect on the level of trust between you and your team. If you're at the top of a large organization, you can imagine the implications for overall performance.

| Value Is Choked

As inaction spreads through the layers, there's a double whammy for your team. The first and most obvious impact is that there's no clear direction to enable people to take action. When you're in wait-and-see mode, it takes no time at all for this to cascade through the layers of people beneath you, and they begin to spend a lot of their time waiting and seeing, rather than doing.

The second impact is that, in the absence of clear direction, people will make it up as they go along—they'll resort to the work that they find most comfortable and enjoyable. Low-value activities creep back in, and any ground you've gained by stripping them out of your work program is lost.

The Accountability Model Is Diluted

Strong, clear, single-point accountability is the foundation of successful execution. When ambiguity prevails, accountability is diluted. Every individual at every level below you has an excuse to sit back and say, "I can't progress my work program until I resolve these critical issues. Until the answers come, I can't do anything." This turns a culture of doing whatever it takes (within ethical and moral boundaries, of course) into a culture of *not my problem.*

The Ambiguity Snowballs below You

If you vacillate on taking decisive action in times of ambiguity, you need to remember that there are many actions below you that will remain unresolved. For example, very early in the COVID-19 crisis, some companies decided to immediately lay off staff, particularly in the travel, hospitality, and tourism sectors. At the time, many people thought this was premature.

But the CEOs who moved most decisively had done their homework: *Here is the most likely outcome of this event. We've made a judgment call on when we think business and recreational travel are likely to return to normal. We've put a lot of effort into modeling the various scenarios for growth in the months and years leading up to a full recovery.* As a result, they took the type of decisive action that may be the difference between their company's long-term survival and its demise.

The key here is simply making the decision. It provides much-needed clarity for those who remain, making the future path clear, and enabling them to remain productive and accountable.

If you don't feel as though you should take decisive action in the face of ambiguity, you'll be tempted to rationalize this in a variety of ways. The most common excuse is *let's wait until we have better information.*

I'm reminded of President Lincoln, who fired the first general-in-chief of the Union Army for inaction, saying, "If General McClellan isn't going to use his army, I'd like to borrow it for a time."

What I've learned over the years is that ambiguity is rarely resolved in the manner you expect it to be, and *never* in the time frame you'd like it to be. You have to take decisive action, regardless of the discomfort and fear you might feel.

Like many things that require self-mastery, you can overcome this anxiety simply by improving your self-discipline. But that's not to say it's easy—it's just simple. We all know how readily we slip back into bad habits, and how difficult it is to embed good ones.

The first step is to understand your own patterns. We delve into this in more depth in the next chapter, but for now just accept that your success will come from letting go of your need for comfort, and embracing discomfort. Just as moving to the next level of leadership inherently forces you into a place of discomfort, taking action in an ambiguous environment does the same. But you don't have to be comfortable with it, you just have to learn to do it.

NO-REGRETS MOVES

Ideally, you resolve ambiguous situations by taking decisive action and keeping your team on a clear course. However, even if you're committed to taking decisive action, sometimes it's simply not possible. This is particularly true if you're at the top of an organization.

Some problems are not only highly ambiguous, but also largely outside your control. Your organization may be deeply affected by issues in the macro environment. On the rare occasion that these arise, they can severely impact your ability to make strategic decisions. This intractable ambiguity can force you to take a wait-and-see approach.

In this kind of scenario, you can't just sit on your hands—you have to find other ways to preserve the momentum of your organization, and deliver value in both the short and long term.

Leading a company in the rapidly evolving energy sector gave me many opportunities to hone my skills in mastering ambiguity. It's worth describing some of these factors before I narrow in on what we did to resolve it.

| Policy Settings

For almost 10 years, successive governments had failed to enact a definitive energy and climate policy. The red and blue flavors of government were philosophically divided, which created havoc for investors. When I first took up my role, there was a price on carbon, which severely limited the profitability of our business. But governments would change every three or so years, and with them the economic conditions for companies like ours. Making investment decisions on assets with a 40- to 50-year operating life is pretty tough when the ground rules you're using to analyze the investment change every few years.

| Ownership Structure

The existing owners of the company were planning to privatize the business within the first 18 months after my arrival. We didn't know whether the transaction would be executed through an IPO, a trade sale, or a split and individual sale of key assets, so we had to be prepared for any eventuality.

| Debt Position

The company's balance sheet was saddled with over $800 million in debt, representing a leverage ratio greater than 65 percent. With market conditions remaining weak, paying down debt and restructuring the balance sheet was a priority.

| Onerous Contract

One of our largest industrial customers held a contract that, for us, was onerous—fulfilling its terms for the life of the agreement would result in a large financial loss. When I came into the business, this future loss was estimated at over $300 million for the decade or so that the contract still had to run.

| Commercial Dispute

The mine that provided the only viable source of coal for our largest power station complex was owned by a large global mining company. It had entered into a long-term contract to provide coal to the power station, and in this case the contract became onerous for *them*. When I became CEO, the contract dispute had already been on foot for almost 10 years. For as long as this issue went unresolved, the predictability of our coal supply would be extremely low. One of the first big decisions of my tenure was to commence litigation against the mine owner to seek enforcement of the contract terms, and provide leverage for a commercial resolution to the dispute.

| Company Culture

The culture in the business had deteriorated over a number of years to be passive, defensive, conformist, dependent, and conflict avoidant. To borrow a term from Peter Senge, the author of *The Fifth Discipline: The Art and Practice of the Learning Organization*, it was a *knowing* culture, rather than a *learning* culture. Knowledge was power, and this power was held by technical specialists—engineers who were focused on technical solutions to technical problems, with little awareness or consideration of commercial outcomes.

Considering this context, I had to put a team in place quickly that could handle this level of complexity and ambiguity. This meant some difficult but decisive choices about people had to be made very quickly.

There were also several ambiguities that we had no control over, which would need to be resolved before we could acquire the certainty we needed to make bigger strategic moves.

In the case of the energy policy vacuum, we had to create two separate asset management and trading plans—one for each set of policy outcomes, depending on which government was in power. These plans were set up flexibly enough to execute very quickly, as the dominant policy emerged. This wasn't an issue on which we could afford to take a wait-and-see approach—we had to work out how to operate in any regulatory and legal context, and plan accordingly. Simple.

When it came to some of the other factors, though, the right answer wasn't quite as clear. Should we invest in building another high-efficiency/low-emission coal-fired power plant? Should we invest in renewable energy plants? Should we sweat our existing assets before looking to expand?

Enter the *no-regrets* move.

Whatever we chose to do had to pass one critical test: regardless of how the prevailing ambiguity was resolved over time, we had to ensure that the value we created was of unquestionable benefit under *any* future scenario. So we put the major asset investment decisions aside, and went back to our basic operations.

| Building the Foundations—Always a No-Regrets Move

To deal with the dysfunctional culture, we started at the very foundations of the organization, building capability in a number of key areas. We freed up a lot of people to be successful in other organizations (which presumably were less interested in commercial competency). We overhauled the company values, the code of conduct, and the leadership performance standards.

We focused on making the company *predictably* safe, overturning decades of poor safety culture by reducing the risks inherent in the work environment. In doing so, we ripped apart arcane policies and processes, replacing them with fit-for-purpose, lean equivalents. We had to completely eradicate the check-box compliance mentality that permeated the culture, replacing it with a singular focus on the things that truly created value.

Most importantly, we grew our human capability by hiring great people who could model the behaviors and performance we were looking for from our leaders. We set a new standard for what leaders do, and started to grow the leadership and commercial talent that could finally extract value from the company's existing technical base.

In any world, this type of foundational work creates value. Irrespective of the external environment, it strengthens the company so that it can respond better to any eventuality it might face in the future. Everything we did in building the foundations improved the company's bench strength—a no-regrets move.

No-Regrets Investing

Although the external environment made it impossible to consider long-term asset investment decisions, which would potentially require multibillion-dollar bets, we understood that our future profitability hinged just as much upon our market trading capability. The expertise and skill to undertake highly complex trading activities was the means by which we monetized the inherent value of our assets in a competitive market.

Our trading capability was solid, not stellar. So we undertook a targeted expansion of capability in both people and systems. Investing tens of millions of dollars into this was a no-regrets move. Regardless of which assets we chose to own and operate in the future, the trading capability to take advantage of them in the financial markets would always create maximum value for the company.

No-Regrets Efficiencies

The culture of complacency produced glaring inefficiencies in both capital expenditure and operating costs throughout the business. Attacking the cost base and implementing new, robust investment criteria took an enormous amount of time, energy, and commitment. Every step of the process was undermined by the silent majority, who wanted to maintain the status quo. Every improvement was hard fought, and the slightest hint of relaxation from leadership saw old habits return almost instantaneously.

It took a number of years, and we went through a lot of senior leaders who simply couldn't shift the culture. The constant battle to strip out cost and break the inertia of the existing culture required us to stop investing in low-value activities. But it was like a game of whack-a-mole—as soon as one blow-out was contained, another would appear. They grew like cancer cells. This constant focus slowed the growth of cost inefficiencies, but I suspect after my five-year tenure there was still plenty of upside left for my successor to pursue!

No-Regrets Insights

I mentioned briefly in Chapter 2 the work we did at one company to bolster our market and customer intelligence, which created a competitive advantage in the sales and marketing process. We did the same here, at a time when ambiguity was at its greatest. We knew that having greater insight into what drove the competitive market, and the scenarios we would most likely have to deal with once the ambiguity was resolved, made our strategic decision-making more reliable. It also gave us incredible confidence when we did take action.

We pursued a deeper understanding of our major customers, uncovering what drove their behaviors. This informed our decisions on how hard we should push back at any point when they sought concessions from us. *You want a deeper discount on your wholesale electricity? Well, that's fine, but in your most recent market announcement you were gloating to your shareholders that you've increased margins from your retail customers in the small to medium enterprise sector by 7 percent. Remind me again why we should give you a cheaper price for your wholesale energy?*

Customer insights can be powerful. Your most sophisticated customers will often use their power and influence to convince you to transfer money from your shareholders' pockets to theirs. Having the right insights is invaluable in this discussion—a no-regrets investment!

No-Regrets Negotiations

In any contract, there are holes, inefficiencies, and imbalances—they're ultimately human documents. Every contract you hold with a major supplier has room for improvement, and this can be a rich source of value. A procurement technique we used was *clean-sheet modeling*, the process of deconstructing an item into its component parts. This enabled some very powerful conversations with some of our suppliers. *We were just wondering how you arrived at the pricing for this part. We're paying $2,425 for each unit, but when we deconstruct the product to look at its individual components, and add the shipping and warehousing costs, it looks like it's only costing you about $416 to deliver to us. What are we missing here?*

Needless to say, a rigorous clean-sheet modeling exercise should lead to beneficial repricing of contracts. This can be done at any time to create value, regardless of the prevailing ambiguity.

No-Regrets Contingencies

Denis Waitley, author of *The Psychology of Winning*, said, "Expect the best, plan for the worst, and prepare to be surprised."

This is important when ambiguity is high. When the dispute with the coal miner that I mentioned previously threatened the quality and quantity of coal we would receive on any given day, we decided to increase our stockpile capacity by over 50 percent. This buffer gave us the flexibility to operate when we chose to, regardless of what our supplier decided to do, regardless of weather events, and regardless of the ongoing legal proceedings.

No-regrets moves aren't simply about marking time until external dependencies are resolved. They are deliberate, high-value actions that preserve your organizational momentum, give your people certainty, and improve the outlook of your business. A no-regrets move will be valuable regardless of if, how, and when the ambiguities in your macro environment are eventually resolved.

AMBIGUITY FOR COMPETITIVE ADVANTAGE

Organizations tend to be insular for the most part. People typically worry about the day-to-day issues of their immediate brief. One of the concepts from the previous chapter that feeds perfectly into mastering ambiguity is the ability to focus on the right time horizon.

For most organizations, strategic planning is an annual activity that fully engages the management team and board of directors for only a short period, and then it's back to running the business.

But if you typically look only to today, this week, and this quarter, your focus will naturally constrain you into short-term thinking. It's only when you learn to shift your focus to the future that you can really consider what's going on outside the confines of your organization. Competitors, market conditions, customer trends, and societal expectations change quickly these days, and can materially affect how you choose to compete.

This is especially the case in times of disaster, disruption, and crisis. We focus inwardly, and forget that strategy is relative, not absolute. It's called competition for a reason—if you don't pay heed to your competitors, you start to think like a monopoly, and your organization can quickly degenerate into a breeding ground for inefficiency, ultimately destroying value for its stakeholders.

But if you have good visibility of the strategic horizon, and a deep understanding of the markets in which you operate, you're likely to see opportunities emerge. This opens up the possibility for you to take advantage of ambiguity when your competitors can't.

During the early days of the COVID-19 crisis, some great examples emerged of organizations that bucked the trend. Rather than simply going into survival mode to weather the economic shocks, they looked to the market for opportunities. Where uncertainty is at its greatest, opportunity abounds—there's a lot of open space to run in.

A great example of a bold competitive move in an ambiguous environment was the gin distillery that, faced with declining revenue from its public tours and gin-making classes, decided to diversify into manufacturing hand sanitizer. The processes and equipment that they had were easily adaptable to a new product, and they were able to take advantage of the short-term spike in demand that couldn't be filled by traditional suppliers. Not only did they compete, but they positioned their hand sanitizer as a boutique, high-end product, with a premium price set accordingly—the product packaging was appropriately fancy.

Personally, I would have expected the demand for gin to massively outstrip the demand for hand sanitizer during a country-wide lockdown. But this company showed great initiative in taking advantage of a shifting competitive environment, with a bold move designed to throw its competitors off balance.

At the same time, the global airline industry was being decimated by border closures and lockdowns. People simply couldn't fly, even if they wanted to. Australia's two major airlines had a very different experience during this time.

Virgin Australia, then led by CEO Paul Scurrah, was saddled with significant debt, and when the revenue suddenly dried up, it wasn't long before the inevitable slide into voluntary administration (the equivalent of Chapter 11 bankruptcy protection). When administrators from Deloitte took control of the airline, tenders were sought for suitable buyers to purchase, restructure, and recapitalize the stricken airline.

Without a viable offer, the airline would cease to exist. So every ounce of energy that the Virgin management team possessed was focused on the airline's survival—seeking financial support from the government and providing support for the administration and sale process. There was no bandwidth to plan bold competitive moves.

Meanwhile, Alan Joyce—CEO of Qantas, Virgin's larger competitor—saw opportunity. He quickly made some decisive announcements. How could he take advantage of his primary competitor's distress and ensure that Qantas gained a lasting competitive advantage from this crisis?

We have to remember that, at this stage, no one had any idea how long border closures would extend, or how long it would be before some normality returned to the global travel industry.

The first things Joyce did were to immediately stand down around 10,000 people, a third of the Qantas workforce, and announce the indefinite closure of certain airline routes. In the space of about three months, he made a number of bold strategic moves that defined Qantas' path forward, rather than letting the ambiguity of the crisis decide its fate.

He undertook a share placement to raise an additional $1.36 billion of capital to ensure the airline had adequate cash reserves to see the immediate crisis through. He announced a three-year plan for the recovery of the airline up to a point where pre-COVID demand was likely to return to the sector, including:

- Reducing costs by $15 billion over the recovery period
- Implementing ongoing costs savings of $1 billion per annum from 2023
- Grounding 100 aircraft for up to 12 months
- Raising additional equity of up to $1.9 billion to accelerate recovery and position Qantas for new opportunities

Joyce also sent a warning shot over the bow of any potential investors in the rebirth of Virgin. He announced that, as soon as Australia's internal borders were reopened, Qantas would be offering airfares between Sydney and Melbourne, the most profitable domestic route in the country, for only $19.

This took advantage of every last ounce of ambiguity to unsettle the Virgin sale process. It said to the bidders, *Be careful what you wish for—you might end up with an airline, but Qantas is going to bring the full force of competition to bear while you're still trying to work out what you've bought—it won't be a smooth ride, so you'd better have deep pockets if you want to play this game.*

Strategically brilliant!

Against all odds, Scurrah led Virgin to be recapitalized after its near-death experience. But it remains to be seen how ready it is to compete with Qantas as the world recovers from the pandemic.

Making the bold moves required to steal a march on your competitors in times of ambiguity, as Joyce did, is one of the distinguishing marks of successful businesses.

The important thing to bear in mind, though, is that seeking competitive advantage in times of ambiguity is not simply an excuse to be cavalier. When ambiguity is at its greatest, the range of possible outcomes is widest—the two bookends that mark the limits between your best-case and worst-case scenarios are much further apart, so it's critical that you know that the organization can withstand that worst case, should it come to pass.

COMMUNICATING CERTAINTY IN AMBIGUITY

When ambiguity is at its greatest, leaders feel as though they should communicate less. It's hard to get in front of your people when you don't have the answers that you think you should. Most leaders avoid communicating at precisely the moment they should be doing more of it.

There is a great truth that, once you understand it, makes it much easier for you to deal with any ambiguity, and communicate confidently to your team: people hate uncertainty way more than they hate bad news.

Uncertainty is debilitating. It makes people speculate, worry, and feel as though they have little or no control. It breeds anxiety and fear, two emotional states that you absolutely don't want infecting your organization. Decisions made through this emotional lens are rarely judicious!

When people get bad news, even if they don't like it, they can actually do something with it. Fear and anxiety recede, and people start thinking about how to respond to the certainty ahead: *Now what do I do?*

The art of storytelling is a critical part of leading through ambiguity. One of my clients, an online women's fashion label, asked me how to best communicate to their organization when COVID-19 hit. Some of their people had to be stood down almost immediately when the impacts of the pandemic became apparent, and those who were left faced an uncertain future.

So we spoke about the story that had to be crafted, which consisted of five very simple points:

1. This is the situation we find ourselves in...

Opening up like this creates context. It's important that people can see the alignment from top to bottom—from the purpose of the organization, right through to the point of understanding what it is they need to do today to make a difference.

Describing the external environment is critical at times like these. *This is what we know... This is what we don't know... This is the immediate impact on the business... These are the decisions we've taken so far... This is why we've made those choices... Here's what we've yet to decide... Here are some of the factors we're watching to shape our decisions...*

Anything you can give people to help them make sense of what's happening in the macro context will make it easier for them to process what they're going through individually. They'll be much more accepting of bad news once they understand a little of the rationale for your choices.

2. This is the prognosis for our business...

In this case, the message was pretty simple: *We've run this business well, and there's absolutely no doubt in our minds that we'll come through this. We may not look the same as we used to, but we'll be better and stronger than we were before the crisis hit.*

A message like this gives confidence, but it needs to be backed up by some facts so that it isn't seen simply as empty motivational rhetoric. Substance is important.

3. Here's our plan for achieving this...

This is the opportunity to provide some substance, with as much information as you can sensibly give. It should support the decisions you're likely to take in the coming months: *We have sufficient cash reserves to survive in our current state until the end of September. If things haven't picked up by then, we'll review it. Until that time, all of you can relax—your jobs aren't under threat.*

The last thing you want is for your people to be worried about being fired, so any certainty you can give them will settle them down, at least enough so that they can focus on what they need to do next. Then you can move on to the specifics: *Here are the steps we're taking to ensure we shape our business to withstand the next six months, regardless of what happens in the external environment. Those things are beyond our control, these things aren't.*

4. Here's what we expect from you...

It's a short step from here to create the call to arms for your people: *If we're going to make this happen, we need your help. Here's what we expect you to contribute, so that we can realize our plan in the coming months.*

This rallying cry should be inspirational, even during the darkest of times. People need to feel accountable for the role they play in handling the crisis, and doing the things that are within their control to the best of their ability.

When done properly, this should empower your people in a way that unleashes their creativity and ingenuity. That's what you want from your people, not having them spend their days sfearing for the future.

5. And here are the opportunities we're pursuing...

We've just looked at the heightened potential for bold strategic moves in times of extreme ambiguity. If you can identify any of these, your people will be invigorated by the prospect of finding growth and opportunity for the business when other businesses are in survival mode. It completely changes the tone of the conversation: *We can see a great opportunity to expand into other market segments. We have the online capability and a loyal community of customers. Now that our competitors have had to close their physical store locations, we can capture some of that market share with our online sales.*

With some very simple tools, you can learn to push through any ambiguity to turn it into an advantage for your team or your organization. The higher up you go, the more influence you'll be able to have over these outcomes, so it's wise to learn to master ambiguity as early in your career as possible.

Developing the discipline to take action with the best available information, rather than being stuck in a waiting game that may never end, is a core requirement of strong leadership. We'll flesh out how to make better decisions in the next chapter, so that you can take action with confidence in any environment.

Once you can combine the wisdom to know when to sit back and wait, with the confidence to pursue no–regrets moves, your leadership potential will skyrocket.

CUTTING THROUGH THE BULLSH!T

In these precarious times, the ability to master ambiguity is more important than ever, regardless of your current leadership level. You have to learn to sit comfortably in ambiguity, and find a way to turn it into certainty for your people. Sometimes it's appropriate to wait, and this is when no-regrets moves come into play. How do you create genuine value, despite having to wait for something beyond your control to be resolved?

For each of the following questions, rate yourself (on a scale of 1 to 10) before you move on to the next chapter. This will give you greater insight into what stands between you and your ability to confidently forge a path for your people through the most ambiguous circumstances.

1. How great is your tendency to freeze when ambiguity is severe?

1 2 3 4 5 6 7 8 9 10

2. How good are you at filtering irrelevant information to chart a clear course of action?

1 2 3 4 5 6 7 8 9 10

3. How well do you communicate the following messages to your people in times of great uncertainty?

• The purpose of the organization

1 2 3 4 5 6 7 8 9 10

• The impact of events on your team

1 2 3 4 5 6 7 8 9 10

• The things you know and don't know, and how they impact your actions

1 2 3 4 5 6 7 8 9 10

• What you need them to focus on to deliver value

1 2 3 4 5 6 7 8 9 10

4. To what extent have you previously relied on no-regrets moves to provide continuity and certainty?

1 2 3 4 5 6 7 8 9 10

5. How easy do you find it to converse with people when you haven't got all the answers?

1 2 3 4 5 6 7 8 9 10

6. How prepared are you to try to drive superior outcomes by making bold decisions?

1 2 3 4 5 6 7 8 9 10

CHAPTER 7

MAKE GREAT

DECISIONS

THE BULLSH!T WE BELIEVE

We've all witnessed the shift in our society to extend greater respect and tolerance to every individual, irrespective of their cultural heritage, their religious beliefs, or their lifestyle. This upheaval is overwhelmingly positive, and provides an essential counterbalance in an increasingly interconnected world.

But in many of our workplaces, we've misinterpreted what the shift to individual rights really means. One of the unintended consequences is that we can be lulled into thinking that *everyone* has the right to be included in the decisions we make.

Not only is this bullshit, it's highly destructive bullshit. Seeking unanimous approval for decisions drives your team into a high-*conformance* culture, not a high-*performance* culture, devoid of the respectful, robust challenge that characterizes great teams. Management by committee becomes the preferred mode of operating, and decision-making by consensus applies the hand brake. It mightn't stop you, but it'll really slow you down.

In this culture, people feel as though they have a right to have their opinions acted upon—but that's simply not the case. A culture of all care, no responsibility is anathema to an efficient, well-run organization where leaders do the jobs they're paid to do. As long as we sit around and talk about how to accommodate every individual's input into a decision, the person who's actually being paid to make decisions isn't doing her job.

Your people's views might be fun and interesting, and I'm not saying that you shouldn't listen to them—quite the opposite, as you'll soon see. But the accountable decision maker is under no obligation to implement every thought that the team utters. Great decisions aren't characterized by unanimous approval—they're characterized by rapid, judicious consideration of all available input (including your people's opinions), followed by choosing a clear course of action. That's how a leader earns her salary.

And you can still bring everyone along on the journey. //

WHAT MAKES A GREAT DECISION?

The most successful organizations are able to out-compete their peers simply because they make better decisions, faster. Better, faster decisions on pricing, cost control, capability building, talent management, capital efficiency, innovation investment… the list goes on.

Decision-making is the culmination of a leader's judgment, experience, and intellect, and you'll see shortly how the leadership capabilities from previous chapters underpin your ability to turn mediocre decisions into great decisions.

But how can you know if your decisions are good, bad, or neutral?

Ultimately, you can only measure the efficacy of your decisions in retrospect. Hindsight illuminates the road as you look back. But there are eight lead indicators you can use prospectively to predict whether a decision you're about to make is likely to be a good one.

1. **Great decisions are timely.**

Speed is probably the most undervalued criterion in great decisions. Timely decisions create momentum, reduce ambiguity, and enable your people to take action. Organizational cadence is determined by the speed of the decisions its leaders make. Fear of making decisions, the reasons for which we'll explore shortly, causes real problems for your people and directly impacts your organization's performance.

But speed doesn't equate in any way to lack of consideration, nor does it imply that you should take a cavalier approach—we're not talking about knee-jerking. When a brisk decision-making tempo is incorporated with the other key factors we're about to discuss, it ensures that your organization can remain agile and responsive to competitive and market forces.

A vast majority of the one-on-one coaching I undertook with my executives was to keep them moving on decisions that they would otherwise procrastinate over. Even the brightest, most experienced executives can tend to take too long over a decision, because they're afraid of the implications of making a wrong one.

2. **Great decisions are made by a clearly accountable person.**
To avoid a consensus culture, there must be clear accountability for every decision that's made, and it has to be abundantly clear to everyone involved who owns that accountability. If you're individually identified as the accountable person, you'll feel a healthy pressure to perform—you're much less likely to slip into avoidance mode. Decision-making rights are linked to accountability with an inseparable bond that should be respected by those above, beside, and below you.

3. **Great decisions are made as close as possible to the core expertise required to make them.**
Having a clearly accountable person is critical, but even this is problematic if it's not the *right* person. Decisions should be made at the lowest practical level—that's the place where the best knowledge, information, and experience reside. There's rarely an occasion when it's a good

idea for you to make a decision that should be made by someone at a lower level.

One of the best decision-making constructs I've had the pleasure of working in was the sales and marketing team I ran for a large freight transportation company. Of the twenty potential B2B customers that we could serve, only six or seven were material. But they each held long-term, high-value contracts with our organization, often worth hundreds of millions of dollars over their life.

The people at the very top of the organization were keenly interested in the outcomes from our negotiations— after all, these contracts were material to the company's ongoing financial prosperity...not to mention shareholder returns and executive bonus payments.

But the top executives weren't the ones who made the decisions—the contract negotiators were. The fact that, hierarchically, the negotiators were three or four levels below the CEO wasn't important—what *was* important is that they were the ones best positioned to make the critical decisions that had to be made. They were the ones who participated in the daily conversations with the customer, observing their reactions to the negotiating pressure points. They were the ones who heard firsthand what the customer valued and what they didn't.

As executives, we made sure that the commercial strategy, risk appetite, and value drivers were clearly defined— but beyond that, our job was to trust and support the negotiators, not to second-guess their judgment. We won those major contracts because we put together outstanding teams, and then let them make the decisions that they were best positioned to make.

4. **Great decisions are shaped by the consideration of many viewpoints.**

Seeking a wide range of expert inputs is a critical part of making great decisions. Of course, the key word here is *consideration*—everyone gets their say, but not everyone gets their way. Consulting with the right people enables you to unlock the power of diversity and tap into the unique talents, viewpoints, and experiences of your people.

Bringing the right people into the loop, eliciting their views, and synthesizing the data into a better understanding of risk and reward is essential for any major decision. You just have to make sure that consideration doesn't come at the expense of accountability and speed.

5. **Great decisions consider the holistic impacts of problems.**

Many decisions are multi-faceted, and the more senior your role, the greater the number of considerations that have to be weighed in every decision. Always try to think beyond the immediate problem at hand to the broader issues. For example, what are the implications of your decision on:

- The strategic context

- Financial performance

- Your organization's reputation and brand

- Customers

- Legal exposure and risk

A great example of this is the decision made many years ago by one of my general managers, Michael, to sack a problem employee. It wasn't a bad decision per se, but he failed to consider the broader implications for the wage negotiations that were on foot. Although Michael's bias to action was commendable, the timing of the decision couldn't have been worse.

The workforce was spooked by the sacking, and it colored the remainder of the negotiations—not at all helpful. Michael's desire to solve his immediate problem caused him to ignore its potential repercussions. It wouldn't have taken much thought, and only a couple of conversations, for Michael to become more circumspect.

6. **Great decisions balance long-term and short-term value.**
There's an increasing trend toward short-termism in many fields. The average longevity of a CEO in a listed company is around five years, so it's little wonder they become engrossed in the pursuit of their short-term financial incentives. Even so-called long-term incentives rarely have a vesting period of greater than three years. How does that affect a CEO's decision to invest in a potential new opportunity that they know may not show strong profitability for several years? That same money could be used to grow an existing cash cow. It's no wonder innovation suffers in many large organizations—the incentives drive a different outcome.

In the case of the wage negotiations we just considered, we ultimately had to make more concessions than we otherwise would have, in order to avoid strike action by the workforce. These concessions solved the immediate industrial relations issue (the short term), but also built less competitive cost structures into the business (the long term).

7. **Great decisions address the root cause of a problem, not just the symptoms.**
Many people rush to solve a problem by eliminating the symptom, but this is like putting a band-aid over a melano-

ma. The problem won't actually go away, because you didn't address the root cause. Often, you need a two-pronged approach: stop the hemorrhaging by treating the immediate symptoms, and work out what needs to be done to ensure the problem doesn't resurface.

In industries where profitability hinges on the availability of key assets (for example, a conveyer belt on a mine site, or a spray painter on a production line), it can be tempting to resolve a symptom quickly to get it operating after it fails. But if you do this repeatedly, you reach a point where machines are held together with spit and gaffer tape, impacting reliability. Ensuring that an asset doesn't fail in the first place is a much cheaper and more effective strategy than becoming a slave to the fail-and-fix cycle. But it's harder to achieve, because it requires investigation and treatment of the root cause.

8. Great decisions are communicated well to your stakeholders.

Being able to communicate a major decision to your key stakeholders in an appropriate manner is the acid test for any decision. Your goal in communicating a decision is not to justify it, to seek approval for it, or to mollify the dissenters. This is your opportunity, in lieu of seeking decision consensus, to bring everyone along with you. We'll look at specifically how to do this at the end of the chapter.

If you can master these decision-making factors, you'll soon find yourself making better decisions, faster. In the world of large B2B sales, the decision-making tempo is often driven by the speed of negotiations, which can extend for over a year, but on occasion can become much more pressing. In one instance, a customer we were attempting to wrest from our major competitor offered us the contract, and wanted to have it finalized in the week between Christmas Day and New Year's Day, in order to meet a market disclosure deadline.

What would normally take several months to achieve, we did in a week. We were able to achieve this speed because we'd already consulted widely with our experts to understand the value drivers. We had undertaken long-term modeling over the 10-year contract life, and examined what-if scenarios to better inform our decisions. We'd fed that all into our decision-making framework, which our negotiators clearly understood. We kept senior stakeholders informed, and only escalated issues for approval where they exceeded our remit.

We made the right decisions for the right reasons at the right time, and it allowed us to capture a disproportionately high percentage of the business we pursued.

SPEED OVER ACCURACY

As the speed of business and competition continues to escalate, our ability to cope relies on how quickly we can respond. Shifts in competitor activity, industry structure, technology, and labor market dynamics now impose a pressing need to stay ahead of the game. Be agile, fail fast, fail cheap.

But despite the fact that we now have virtually limitless tracts of data to support us, the process of decision-making remains very *human*. We still hesitate because of our fear of getting it wrong. We agonize over the potential personal impacts that making a poor decision might bring. We think about what *others* might think about our decision.

No one wants to make mistakes, which is why a shift in your mental approach is the most critical step to improving your decision-making speed and competence. The one thing that will do the most to improve your decision-making speed is realizing that *not making a decision is more damaging than making a less-than-perfect decision.*

The whole concept of speed has changed as a result of the COVID-19 pandemic. Prior to the various stay-at-home orders imposed across the world, it would have taken months, maybe even years for an organization to plan, implement, and adapt to remote working protocols and technologies. But in order to survive and continue to operate, many companies managed to achieve this in a matter of days.

This shows that your decisions don't need to be perfect, they need to be *excellent.* Having the experience to know when you reach that point of excellence—the point of diminishing returns—is where your judgment comes into play. The risk of any decision determines how much latitude you have. In most cases, your decisions just need to be *roughly* right, not absolutely right.

Let's look at a couple of examples from professional sports. The Professional Golfers Association (PGA) tour is a great example where consistency of outcomes is critical. It's also a sport where being roughly right works pretty well. When a professional golfer tees off in a tournament, they're trying to land the ball on the fairway, that beautiful piece of groomed turf that provides the perfect surface and position for their next shot.

How often do you think the top golf professionals actually do what they're aiming to do, and land the ball on the fairway? Well, according to PGA Tour statistics, the top five players in 2019 had an average accuracy of just over 60 percent. Think about it—four times out of 10, the ball doesn't go exactly where they want it to… and these are the best players in the world, earning millions of dollars.

Major League Baseball (MLB) is the same. A professional baseball player knows that each time he steps up to the plate, the odds are against him getting to first base. In fact, if he only manages to get on base one-third of the time—once every three at-bats—and does that consistently over the course of his career, he would be amongst the top 30 MLB players of all time.

If you can genuinely understand this, and apply it to your work context, you might feel a little more comfortable in making decisions quickly—despite the ambiguity, in the absence of all the desired information, and without the unanimous agreement of your people.

A decision made today that's 80 percent right is infinitely better than a decision made in three weeks' time that's 85 percent right... which is infinitely better than a decision made in two months' time that's 90 percent right.

Instilling a Decision-Making Discipline

When a crisis occurs, particularly one that attracts external scrutiny, you don't get to choose the timing of your decisions. You're forced to respond to the tempo set by, say, a regulatory enquiry, a media investigation, or an existential threat.

Most people who find themselves in crisis situations tend to get by. They make decisions as quickly as the situation dictates, and they get things done. Whether they're good decisions is another matter. But they keep moving until they can fall back into the comfortable space of being able to ruminate indefinitely over every decision.

A number of years ago, the CEO of the rail freight business I was working for asked me to act in his place while he and a number of more experienced executives took a well-earned Christmas break. But what I thought would be a nice opportunity to warm the CEO's chair and enjoy the view from his office quickly turned into a full-blown crisis. A major weather event caused widespread flooding of the river systems, towns, and infrastructure in our main operating regions.

The lion's share of our revenue came from the rail services and infrastructure that we provided to transport coal from the mines to the ports. Each train carried up to 10,000 tons of coal, and this infrastructure was critical in supporting one of Australia's largest export industries. Rail lines were closed, and in some cases severely damaged, as they became submerged in the rising floodwaters.

The pressure to make decisions quickly was intense, but I had a lot of support around me to do so, including a very experienced board of directors and a CEO who, instead of sunning himself on the beaches of Hawaii, spent countless hours on the phone.

The most interesting decisions came when trying to decide what information should be released to shareholders via the Australian Securities Exchange. Disclosure obligations are not as black-and-white as you might imagine, and revising earnings guidance too early can create more problems than leaving the original guidance in place. We knew there would be a significant financial impact, but until the waters receded and we could properly assess the damage, our estimates could easily have been off by tens of millions of dollars.

The key to our success here was to make decisions quickly, and then retest them at short intervals. *We decided yesterday that it would be inappropriate to release revised earnings guidance to the market. Has anything changed since then that would cause us to reconsider this decision?*

My stint in the CEO's chair was very brief, after which I led a task force to oversee the company's full recovery.

This crisis was like attending a master class on how to make big, high-value decisions quickly, and it led me to ask myself some important questions: *If I can make sound decisions this quickly in a crisis, why can't I do it all the time? Which elements enabled us to make great decisions under pressure, and how can I replicate them without the catalyst of a crisis?*

For the last decade, I've progressively refined the discipline that helps me to keep tabs on my decision-making speed. Making faster decisions is absolutely achievable without sacrificing the elements that underpin their soundness.

| Tracking Your Decisions

Even if you don't think you have a problem, try this for a few months. First, ask your people about your decision-making pace—you might be surprised by what you learn. There's no better way to start anything than by boosting your self-awareness!

Tracking your decisions will help to ensure you don't inadvertently become a roadblock for your people. Always look to explicitly record the decisions you have to make, and keep track of them. For every major decision, apply the discipline of recording these few key pieces of data:

- What's the specific decision that you're accountable for making?

- When did you first become aware that you had to make this decision?

- Who else is dependent on the decision you're making?

- What are you waiting for (information, people, events, etc.)?

- When do you expect the things you're waiting for to materialize?

- What if they never materialize?
- What's the drop-dead date for making this decision?
- What's the potential impact of any delay to making this decision?
- What's the potential downside if you were to make a decision today?

You may be quite surprised at the answers to these questions, once you start to track them consistently. It's incredibly easy for a few weeks to slip by while you're buried in other critical issues. That's why it's so important to constantly ask the question, *Who else is dependent on the decision I'm making?*

Remember, it's speed over accuracy, every time. If you want to maintain any sort of tempo and momentum in your team, this is what it takes. Without the basic self-awareness that comes from having a decision-making discipline, I've seen many smart executives put a wall of uncertainty up in front of their teams. Motivation and productivity decline, and confusion reigns. But how do you make faster decisions without compromising quality?

Excellence over perfection is a core principle of making great decisions quickly. You have to know when enough data is enough, when enough consultation is enough, when enough analysis is enough, when enough brainstorming is enough, and when enough deliberation is enough. These are all micro decisions that you need to take on your way to making a great decision.

FILTERING THE NOISE

Whenever you're faced with a major decision, there will be dozens of data points to consider. Some of these will be pushed to you by a person who believes their perspective is the most important thing in the world.

I recall a difficult pricing decision for a customer that had asked us to enter into a cheap, long-term electricity supply contract, knowing that we valued the certainty a contract like that would bring. But there was a major sticking point: there was a chasm between the price our customer wanted, and the price that we were prepared to offer.

From the customer's perspective, they knew all too well what an important player they were in the market. They were a major employer, generated significant economic activity, and were a highly respected brand. On the basis of their sheer scale alone, they could have rightly expected some preferential treatment in pricing.

Unfortunately, they overestimated the value that we would gain from having contractual certainty, as the price pushed us into an economically unviable position.

Politicians and local business owners alike wanted to see a deal done to ensure the long-term viability of our customer, and of course the employment and economic growth that went hand-in-hand with their operations.

We wanted to ensure that the customer continued to operate profitably, but we weren't prepared to do so at significant expense to our shareholders by negotiating an economically irrational deal.

When we pared back the noise, there were only a few factors that were genuinely relevant to our decision:

- Offering the price sought by our customer would destroy economic value for our company's owners

- The media barrage wouldn't stop, even if we made some modest concessions

- Our customer's choices on how they ran their operations were theirs to make, and it would be totally inappropriate for us to feel accountable for them

All of the other variables—the potential loss of employment, the media hype, the politicians' exhortations, the possible reputational repercussions—were all just noise. They were compelling noise, but noise all the same. Once we focused on the obligations and duties we had to our shareholders, it made everything else much easier. We discarded the extraneous information, and made the right decision by balancing our fiduciary responsibilities with the potential impacts on our broad array of stakeholders.

STEPS FOR EFFECTIVE FILTERING

You can learn the skill of filtering information to make any decision more manageable. It's a process of eliminating data by looking at it dispassionately, and determining its relevance. To do this, you need to be able to explore the inputs calmly and unemotionally, which is not always easy when the people closest to you have opposing but strident views.

A no bullshit leader will determine the critical factors in a decision, and remove everything else from their deliberations. They'll take counsel from experts who can add value to those dimensions, and not be distracted by the many voices whose opinions aren't relevant. There's a simple process for filtering out the noise and whittling down the multitude of factors to something more manageable.

1. **Start with reference to your values.**
The easiest distraction to remove from a major decision is any option that would contravene your values. For example, if you were to discover a case of embezzlement, bribery, or

corruption in your team, the option to cover it up and hope that no one notices isn't a valid option. Get rid of it.

I've seen some very senior leaders cover up major breaches in values and behaviors, sometimes bordering on criminal conduct, to avoid the inevitable backlash and scrutiny that would follow from the board, the shareholders, or the wider community. They spend a lot of time wrestling with what to do, and often end up making bad decisions for the wrong reasons. This is the thin edge of the wedge. Once you normalize the departure from your moral and ethical values, team culture deteriorates.

2. Stop agonizing over the cold hard facts.

We know that some things can't be changed. You should seek only to understand the impact they can potentially have on your decision—then move on quickly. Cold hard facts shouldn't occupy any of your energy in decision-making.

3. Recognize and eliminate self-interest.

A great decision is one in which you've been able to put aside your self-interest and make the decision purely in the best interests of the organization. This is really hard. Would you be prepared to cancel a project that you knew was value-destructive if it meant you would be out of a job? Would you change the classification of safety incidents in order to meet your KPIs? Would you inappropriately capitalize costs in order to meet short-term financial targets and earn your bonus?

Ask yourself the question, *What if my life depended on making the* right *decision?* This paradoxically removes any thought of self-interest by engaging the greatest driver of self-interest (survival) and focusing on the greater good. It frees you up to make the best decision for the organization, not for yourself. It also earns a lot of respect and trust with the team, in the same way self-interest destroys it. Remember, once your people see that you're in it for yourself, they'll never be in it for you. Ever.

4. Look for conflicts of interest.

It's highly likely that some of the people providing input to your decisions are close to you, and therefore know how to influence your thinking. Sometimes, you'll have friendships with people you're afraid to upset by making a decision that they either won't like or won't agree with.

While you examine your decision-making inputs, ask yourself these questions: *Am I worried about upsetting someone? Do I have a relationship with someone who'll benefit from my decision? Do I have an emotional investment in any particular outcome?*

5. Work out if you're afraid of anything.

Quite often, your fears will drive you to examine soft options and compromises that aren't in the best interests of the organization. If decision-making is driven by fear, you'll always follow the path of least resistance. Recognizing your fears will help you to put that aside, and to follow the mantra, *I'll make the right decision, for the right reasons, without hesitation—because it's right.*

6. Rank the decision-making criteria by relative importance.

Once you've eliminated the obvious distractions using the first five steps, you can then get back to the discipline you already know—value ranking. By the time you get to this point, you should have a reasonably manageable set of criteria. With the few remaining criteria, you can then rank them (e.g., from 1 to 6, or 1 to 24, etc.) in order of importance. If you can focus on the top criteria (of which there might be just three or four), the field of possible choices is narrowed very quickly.

Making any decision more manageable by focusing on the most relevant inputs will facilitate everything else you do. It'll reduce the number of stakeholders you need to consult, and the amount of input required from your advisors. It'll reduce the amount of data you need to analyze, because it will be limited to only those inputs that remain after you've filtered out the noise.

Better decisions, faster!

LIBERATING YOUR PEOPLE'S TALENT

True value in diversity is unlocked by harnessing the unique perspectives, experiences, capabilities, and ideas that your people bring. Having a diverse team is important (for moral reasons, if nothing else), but if you want to actually make use of that diversity, you have to truly engage and include each individual.

How can you get the most out of your people and liberate their talent, without allowing yourself to slip into decision-making by consensus? To encourage people to contribute to any given decision, you not only need to give them a seat at the table, but you also have to make it safe for them to express their views. Establishing a culture where robust challenge and debate is not just accepted, but *expected*, is a critical piece of this puzzle.

As I would often say to the executives who worked for me, "If you think the same as me, then at least one of us is redundant...and it probably isn't me!"

We love it when people agree with us and tell us how smart and insightful we are. Even the best of us are susceptible to fawning and flattery, and some people are expert at giving it without seeming the least bit insincere. These are called yes-men (or women), and I'm sure you've been seduced by them at some stage in your career. This weakens your ability to make good decisions because your own views are reinforced regardless of their true merit.

Another one to watch out for is the introverted expert. They often don't have the confidence to speak out or contradict a peer in a group forum, preferring to keep their own counsel. Sometimes they'll remain silent, never giving you the benefit of their views (which they'd rather reserve for close colleagues in quiet corners). Other times they'll approach you one-on-one to express their opinion. Either way, they're not helping you to explore the merits of different viewpoints, because they're not engaging in debate.

Getting the right people in the room is a good start, but how do you get the right *information* into the room? First, stop doing dumb shit. It's amazing how leaders (including me, I might add) can unwittingly stifle conversation and debate. You'll never get the best from your people this way. Here's six surefire ways to stop killing the conversation, and promote healthy debate:

1. Qualify the room.

Only people who can add value to a decision should be in the room, and this is usually fewer people than you think (or *they* think). People love having input in an all care, no responsibility way, but that's not constructive. It slows the process down and adds little value to the outcome. It also leads to the most insidious of weapons: the power of veto. Get the right people in the room, give them all the information they need to fully contribute to the topic, and create an environment where it's easy for them to express their views.

2. Don't speak first.

Here's what I think… Now tell me what you think. Only the most robust and forthright of your people will express an opinion that's inconsistent with your views. If you speak first, you set the tone for what's expected from everyone else. It's the most obvious way to stifle healthy challenge, so try not to do it, even if it's painful to remain silent when listening to some people's opinions. It'll not only enhance your eventual decision, but you'll also learn a lot about the capability of your people along the way.

3. **Listen objectively.**

I've often observed leaders showing signs of anger or impatience when someone expresses a view they don't like. This teaches people to think carefully about how their input will be received. Often, the moment will pass them by while they're weighing up the pros and cons of making a contribution. Worse still, they may decide that the safest course of action is to say nothing. A real culture killer.

4. **Draw in the quiet ones.**

Many of your people won't feel comfortable expressing their views in a group forum. But if they want to perform effectively in their role, they're going to have to get over that. Help them to contribute by observing their reactions to certain statements, and ask them by name to contribute when you think they might have something useful to add. *Christine, I know you have some good ideas about valuing our customers' solvency risk—what's your view on Peter's proposal?*

5. **Demonstrate a willingness to shift.**

People will work out fairly quickly if you're simply going through the motions of consultation. When excellent counterpoints are made, or new information is exposed, you should demonstrate a willingness to shift your views accordingly. If you remain steadfast in your opinions, despite better information being revealed, people will see that you don't really value their opinions, and they'll stop offering them.

6. Encourage robust debate.

As long as it remains respectful, robust debate is essential in good decision-making. If your people can wrestle with issues and understand the counter-balance of value in opposing viewpoints, the eventual decision will be much more reliable. When differing viewpoints emerge, encourage the debate. Step back and summarize the opposing perspectives, and ask other people what they think of the dilemma. I've seen this technique reap tremendous value in a team setting. But you, as the leader, have to be completely comfortable in the conflict that emerges when two passionate proponents have opposing viewpoints.

Liberating your people's talent is an essential part of making great decisions, and it's the only way to truly harness the diversity in your team. But inclusion, consultation, and collaboration should never come at the expense of strong accountabilities for decision-making.

Weak leaders will try to push their accountability onto the group and seek consensus. Strong leaders will work tirelessly to acquire the right input quickly, and then make a decision. A great decision will be summarized by the accountable decision-maker like this: *OK, thanks very much everyone for your input; it's been extremely valuable. I've heard everything you've said, and your viewpoints have helped to shape my thinking on the issues at hand. Now here's what we're going to do, and we're going to do it for these reasons. Here's what I need you all to do now to execute this decision.*

This approach can unlock untold value, and still bring your people along with you as you decisively resolve issues and create momentum for your team.

COMMUNICATING MAJOR DECISIONS

In the preceding chapter, we looked at how to communicate with certainty in a world of ambiguity. When it comes to communicating major decisions, the same principles apply.

Why would you bother to communicate a decision to your people? More than anything, you want them to know that you're a rational decision maker who can be relied upon to sensibly guide the team. It builds their trust and confidence, even if they don't always agree with you. It also helps to create alignment and consolidate their commitment to delivering the outcomes from any decision.

You need to be a little careful, though—when you communicate a decision, you're *not* looking for people's approval. You're not apologizing for your decision, nor are you trying to sway people to your point of view. You don't need to justify your decision to anyone (except perhaps your boss, if she asks).

Several underlying messages should shine through when you communicate any decision. Without stating them explicitly, it should be obvious to everyone how your mind works when you make a major decision:

- I'll act according to my values, and the values of the organization.

- I'll put self-interest aside, and decide on the basis of what's best for the organization.

- I'll listen carefully to the people around me, and can be influenced by their views.

- I'll weigh up all relevant factors quickly, but carefully.
- I'll make what I believe is the right decision, even at the risk of being unpopular.

Ultimately, though, people will view your decisions through their own lens, not yours. You have broader access to information than anyone in your team, not least of which is the input you receive from above. And as you take on increasingly senior roles, it becomes even more obvious that your decisions won't please everyone...so you might as well just do the right thing!

Communicating a Failure

When I took up the CEO role at a large energy utility some years ago, I inherited a project called Solar Boost. This project was putting into trial a new technology in solar thermal electricity generation, which would feed into one of our existing power stations, which just happened to be the newest, most efficient coal-fired power station in the market.

The theory was that a new facility would be built to reflect the sun's power using thousands of mirrors, which would super-heat and pressurize steam. This would then be used to drive the huge turbine already in place at the power station, generating clean, green electricity. It would be a renewable substitute for coal, replacing about 5 percent of the station's overall capacity.

It was good in theory, and by the time I arrived, a lot of progress had already been made. But there were some very significant issues. The technology that was supposed to be leading-edge turned out to be *bleeding*-edge—it was unproven in the conditions and context we were trying to use it in. The technology provider was somewhat immature, and our own project management discipline and capability were poor.

The project was in the construction phase. A large area adjacent to the power plant had been cleared, the civil engineering work had been completed, and the massive steel frames that would house the thousands of mirrors had been erected. Every day when they arrived at the site, our people could see the march of progress. This was our future—a renewable alternative to coal. In many ways, the project was a beacon of hope for the company.

The only problem was, it was never going to work. The project was economically marginal from the start, and the problems and setbacks we experienced along the way had pushed it deeply into value-destructive territory. Just before I arrived, the contractor had abandoned the site as a result of the brewing commercial impasse.

So here we were—a site well underway in the construction phase, 5,700-odd giant mirrors that had been fabricated and delivered to site, millions of dollars of project investors' money sunk, a high risk of integration failure with the main plant (even if we *did* complete the project), and no path to an even remotely acceptable commercial outcome.

Ultimately, the board approved our recommendation to cancel the project.

There was nowhere to hide—it was a failure of epic proportions. The project had widespread visibility in the market because of the innovative technology being deployed in what was a key part of the company's strategic transition to a brighter future.

But even if there was an opportunity to hide the project's demise, we wouldn't have. An essential part of making great decisions is owning the outcomes of those decisions, for better or for worse. Trying to gloss over poor decisions or rewrite history is the refuge of weak leaders. Strong leaders own the outcomes, without any spin or bullshit.

The problem then remained—how could we communicate this decision to our people? From the outside, the project looked almost complete. No one knew of the incredible risk posed to the existing multibillion-dollar power plant. They didn't know that the global company providing the technology had announced a complete withdrawal from its solar thermal business. They didn't know that to complete the project would require an additional $50 million, pushing the project losses to catastrophic levels.

So we told them.

THE POWER OF STORYTELLING

Communicating through stories is by far the most effective way to reach people. Explaining the background, the key events, and some of the factors that drove our decision-making along the way was instrumental in gaining understanding and acceptance of our decision to terminate the Solar Boost project.

1. Give some context.

Giving context helps people to understand the baseline against which everything else can be measured. It brings people's knowledge to a common level, and primes them for the story that you'll reveal.

Let's be clear on why we initially embarked on this project. It was a demonstration project to determine whether or not this new technology was technically and commercially viable. It fitted very well into our strategy to move away from coal as a fuel source for generating electricity, and reduce our carbon footprint. We knew there would be many risks, and the original investment was approved with full knowledge of these. Unfortunately, many of the anticipated risks (and others that were never imagined) materialized during the course of the project, making the marginal business case completely untenable.

2. **Talk through the history.**

Talking through key events chronologically helps to remind people of the chain of events that led to your decision. It also brings out the most material aspects of the saga, elevating your team's gaze above the minor or immaterial events that were of little consequence in your decision. It reinforces the filtering of information we mentioned earlier in this chapter.

Logistics issues plagued the supplier from the start. Even the relatively routine exercise of shipping equipment to the site suffered major delays and setbacks. One of our supplier's key subcontractors fell into financial distress and eventual liquidation, which created further delays. By the time we were able to examine some of the components, we discovered that they weren't manufactured to the quality standards that we thought had been agreed upon in the contract. The dispute deepened, and the fundamental specifications of the project came into question. This resulted in further delays, and the project fell hopelessly behind schedule.

3. **Explicitly outline the things you can and can't say.**

Often, you won't be able to reveal everything in a communication to your people, as you'd reasonably expect that anything you say could appear on the front page of the local newspaper. Explaining what you can't say, and why, sometimes fills important gaps in the story, and further improves the trust that the communication generates.

Clearly, I can't go into any details of our negotiations with the supplier, as they're commercial-in-confidence. What I can say is that we've reached a financial settlement, and the project has now been terminated.

4. **Explain the main options you examined (and discarded).**

Although everyone will have an opinion on how you could have solved the problem differently, give them a flavor of which credible options you explored, and why you arrived at your ultimate decision.

There were no good options here. To proceed with the project would mean that we'd have to take on all project risk and work out how to integrate the technology ourselves, without the support of our original supplier. The risk would have been intolerable, but even if we leave this point aside, we still would have had to invest at least another $50 million in order to complete the project. Despite the investment we had already sunk into the project, we couldn't put good money after bad.

5. **Explain your decision clearly.**

Make sure people understand what the decision actually is and, having now made it, how you feel about it. This will help them to see that no decision of this magnitude is easy, and there will always be trade-offs.

We made the decision to terminate the project, and this has now been approved by the board. It was simply not reasonable to continue a project that, even in the best-case scenario, would cause us to lose substantial amounts of shareholder money. The risk to the existing plant was also not something we were prepared to entertain, given that this power station is the company's premier asset. I know that many of you will be disappointed with this outcome, but this was the only responsible decision we could make.

6. **Outline the next steps and what you need from your people.**

Now that the decision has been made, what does this mean for the people and the organization?

Unwinding a project of this magnitude is never simple. What you'll notice immediately is that there's likely to be some reports of the project cancelation in the media. You'll also see that the company will write off the investment made to date, and that will appear in our annual report. The Solar Boost site will need to be remediated at some point to remove the structures that have been built, but this isn't our main priority right now. Remember, over 5,700 mirrors will need to be destroyed, and I don't want to be the CEO to do that, just in case the superstition of attracting seven years of bad luck for breaking a mirror is actually true. That would send about 40,000 years of bad luck my way.

A little humor doesn't hurt at times like this.

Communicate as honestly and openly as you possibly can, and give people some insight into what issues caused you the most difficulty and uncertainty while you were making the decision. Don't pretend a complex decision was simple, or that you had all the answers when you made it. This is almost never the case with decisions at the highest levels of organizations.

Making decisions requires your judgment, experience, and intellect. Making *great* decisions also requires the right temperament and a commitment to work fearlessly to get the right information on the table. This means you need to be courageous enough to discard any information that isn't material, regardless of who's trying to convince you it is. It means you have to know how to get the most out of your people, and you must manage the conflicts that inevitably arise when you promote a culture of robust challenge and debate. It means you have to practice what you preach—excellence over perfection, speed, and personal accountability.

It won't be easy, but if you can learn to make better decisions faster than your competitors, and build this into your organization's DNA, your organization will gain a true competitive advantage.

CUTTING THROUGH THE BULLSH!T

Although there are many excellent decision-making frameworks available, you need to go beyond them if you want to be a great decision maker. Will you discipline yourself to make decisions faster than you think you could? Are you prepared to create a culture where people feel safe to give you their genuine opinion? Are you strong enough to say *no* to people who want to provide input, but don't possess the necessary expertise? Will you stand back and let the accountable person make decisions, whether they do it your way or not?

For each of the following questions, rate yourself (on a scale of 1 to 10) before you move on to the next chapter. This will give you greater insight into what stands between you and your ability to make better decisions, faster.

1. How do you rate your decision-making speed?

2. How do you think your people would rate your decision-making speed?

3. How comfortable are you in making a decision without enough data to support you?

4. To what extent do you seek to influence the people below you who are making decisions?

5. How well do you think you maintain a long-term value focus when making decisions?

6. How widely do you consider the impacts of your decisions on stakeholders?

7. How comfortable are you making unpopular decisions?

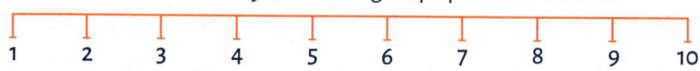

8. How do you rate your ability to draw out the best from the diverse expertise in your team?

CHAPTER 8

DRIVE ACCOUNTABILITY

THE BULLSH!T WE BELIEVE

The trend toward autonomous teams, flatter organizational structures, and collaborative workspaces is supposed to liberate new levels of innovation and creativity from your people. In theory, if you stand back and let people do what they do best, everything will come together organically. You'll get much better results because people are smart, and they'll work it out. Any interference from management is just that—interference.

This theory neglects the fact that *nothing happens unless a leader makes it happen.* Nurturing cultures are nice, but there's one very important precondition for execution excellence that you need to create: strong, single-point accountability. One head to pat, one arse to kick!

Accountability is the vital counterbalance to collaboration. When people collaborate, they look for ways to fit together and integrate their ideas, which is a good thing. But they also spend a lot of time making compromises and concessions. This might work in a few extreme outlier organizations like the Silicon Valley unicorns, which arguably harbor the best and brightest talent on the planet. But for the overwhelming majority of firms, any upside from broad-based collaboration is more than offset by the downside of confusion and inefficiency that a weak accountability culture creates.

When people seek consensus from their peers (who may or may not have a valuable contribution to make), time slips away. Value disintegrates. The previous chapter laid out why your decisions need to favor speed over accuracy. They need to be made quickly, and they need to be roughly right. As more information comes to light after the fact, you can adjust as you go. Excellence over perfection.

Accountability is the bedrock that execution excellence is built upon. For every major outcome in your organization, you need a single accountable person who's empowered to make whatever decisions are necessary to achieve that outcome. It's the only way to optimize results.

Single-point accountability is everything, and it's the real catalyst for releasing your people's creativity, energy, and commitment. //

ONE HEAD TO PAT, ONE ARSE TO KICK

Most larger organizations have a reasonable strategy. These strategies look eminently sensible in the PowerPoint presentations to investors, and the glossy posters adorning the walls of the head office. So what separates the exceptional performers from the also-rans? They *execute* really well. And execution takes leadership—the type of strong leadership that brings clarity to ambiguity, and decisiveness to hesitation.

The individual who's ultimately answerable for an activity or deliverable is said to hold the *accountability* for that activity. Although there may be many people who are responsible for delivering different components, there can only be one person who's accountable for the overall result.

We all need to feel the weight of accountability to bring out our best. When you know that you alone are accountable for achieving an outcome, the task takes on new meaning. Without this, an attitude of all care, no responsibility dominates, and when this attitude is multiplied through many people and organizational layers, it becomes a pervasive culture. There's no real pressure on you to perform, because there will always be someone else who's equally responsible for the work—you can always shift the blame to them if things don't go to plan.

That's why *shared accountability is no accountability.* Without single-point accountability, a lack of ownership kills the drive for results. And a lack of drive dramatically affects the time, quality, and cost of any deliverable. Gaps form that otherwise wouldn't, and you create the perfect environment for duplication of effort.

One of the most memorable examples of a shared account-ability failure in my career was in the planning of a major overhaul at one of my company's power stations. Typically, these overhauls would be planned 12 to 18 months in advance. They would cost somewhere between $40 million and $80 million, and funding would be progressively sought in tranches, as various stage gates were passed and the scope of the work was refined.

For this overhaul, we'd engaged an external supplier to provide the specialized labor force for the shutdown. Our standing workforce of around 100 people would swell to over 500 for a few months while the work was being carried out, before we reverted to our normal operational staffing levels.

At one point, a decision had to be made on the turbine, the most critical component of the power station, with a number of complex technical and commercial considerations. To make this decision, we held a workshop at our head office with expert engineers, project managers, our external supplier, and executives of the business. There were over 40 people in a conference room, spending the better part of a day wrestling with the issues to select the best option.

I remember talking to the accountable executive at the end of the day to ask whether they'd achieved the desired outcome. He was extremely happy with how the workshop had progressed. The level of cooperation between our people and our labor supplier had deepened. We'd honed our clarity of purpose. And, most importantly, everyone had agreed on the optimum solution for the turbine.

A couple of days later, I heard along the grapevine that the solution agreed at the workshop had been overruled by Ron, the engineering manager at the power station in question. Apparently, Ron didn't agree with the decision, and wanted to implement a different option.

Without casting any judgment as to who was right and who was wrong, this provoked a few obvious questions:

1. If Ron was accountable for this decision, why wasn't he leading the workshop?

2. If Ron wasn't accountable for this decision, then who was?

3. How was the decision made in the first place, if there wasn't a clearly accountable person?

4. How can 40-plus people (minus Ron) spin their wheels and burn money without a clearly accountable decision maker to drive the outcomes?

This was one of many examples where people, with the best intent, the best expertise, and all the funding and support they could possibly want, couldn't get an acceptable outcome purely because there wasn't a single accountable individual identified for that project.

I'm going to go out on a limb here: if the only thing you did differently as a leader was to ensure that all your people had clear, single-point accountabilities, and you created a culture and rhythm of adhering to these accountabilities, there would be very few teams that could match your results.

Accountability in a Passive/Defensive Culture

Very few organizations have this nailed, but some suffer more than others from a lack of clear accountabilities. I've experienced on several occasions what happens in cultures with low accountability and high levels of avoidance, dependence, and conformity: people master the art of hiding in plain sight. They all appear to be diligent, committed, hardworking, results-focused individuals. But the lack of accountability, through every layer of the organization, is insidious.

Trying to work out who's accountable for any outcome is like trying to nail jelly to a cloud. *Well, I'm only doing this bit... Greg is doing that bit, and Leanne is doing the other bit. And I'm not sure who's doing the bit that brings it all together.* You can imagine how frustrating it was to try to work out who was delivering the key outcomes for the company.

Things just rolled along, and people were given the benefit of the doubt for trying their best, regardless of the outcome. Late? Over budget? Poor quality? Not fit for purpose? *Hey, don't worry, we all worked hard and we meant well.* Seriously!

Turning this around has to start at the top, with executive accountability. At the very least, you need to be clear on which executive is accountable for any deliverable, but even this isn't as straightforward as it sounds. Because many deliverables span multiple executive portfolios, there's often a tendency to say, "Sorry, Martin, I'm waiting on Jeff's people to do their bit before we can deliver." The only way to address this malaise is to find some new executives who aren't afraid of shouldering their accountability.

Once you work out how to manage executive account-ability, you're then able to further refine down through the layers of leadership until the ultimate accountability lands with the appropriate person at the appropriate level.

Seeing how weak the execution capability was in some organizations I've worked in strongly influenced the way I reshaped the corporate values. There are two schools of thought about how to optimally capture a company's val-ues: *Should the values describe the* existing *culture, behaviors, and preferences that people know and love, or should they describe the* desired *target state, despite the obvious gaps in the existing culture?*

I've always been a believer in the latter. If I'd enshrined the values that underpinned the *existing* culture in several of the companies that I worked in, those values might have been as follows:

- **TOLERANCE**—Everyone has a job, no matter how poorly they behave or perform.

- **EXPERIENCE**—We know our shit, because we've done the same things over and over for decades.

- **TROUBLESHOOTING**—We work tirelessly to fix things when something goes wrong, but we don't focus on pre-venting a failure before it occurs.

- **ENTITLEMENT**—The company owes us a living, and we should be financially rewarded for the slightest discre-tionary effort or improvement.

But in every organization, you'll find pockets of excellence and high performance. That's what keeps companies going, despite the obvious undercurrent of mediocrity.

Often, choosing values that describe the desired future state of a company is the way to begin the conversation about what needs to change. What will guide the organization to lift its performance? I like to use imperative statements as a way of energizing people toward a preferred future state, for example:

- **BE SAFE**—We believe that all injuries are preventable, and we challenge ourselves to find safer, smarter ways of working.

- **CREATE VALUE**—We focus on results. We're constantly looking for better ways to do things, and we maximize the long-term value of the business.

- **TAKE ACCOUNTABILITY**—We're accountable for our own contribution and the results we deliver. We own our failures, accept responsibility, learn, and grow, getting better as we go.

- **ACT WITH INTEGRITY**—We challenge each other, constructively and respectfully. We do what we say we'll do. We're honest and trustworthy, always acting in the company's best interests.

When you start off, these values aren't going to be particularly representative of the average employee. But the *right* employees will love that this is where you're taking the company.

A culture that's founded on strong, single-point accountabilities will outperform one that isn't. Accountability is not only best for the organization and its many stakeholders, but also for every individual who has the opportunity to work in that environment. Once embraced, what initially appeared daunting unlocks people's potential, allowing them to feel the satisfaction that can only come from achieving difficult goals.

BENEFITS OF A STRONG ACCOUNTABILITY CULTURE

In the preceding chapter we looked at the problems created if accountability for decisions isn't clearly established. Decision-making by consensus, and the de facto power of veto that often accompanies it, will stymie progress and slow the tempo of the organization to glacial speed. What, then, are the benefits of a strong accountability culture?

1. **It improves individual performance.**

When an individual holds clear decision rights, and everyone around them knows it, the tone of every conversation changes. Their motivation to deliver is amplified, and they become much more proactive in every area of their remit. They take on the onus for making whatever decisions are necessary to ensure their milestones are met. They report accurately on progress, because they know in the end they'll own any failures, regardless. They find the gaps and overlaps that would inevitably form without the benefit of them taking full ownership.

But a word of caution here. Even though single-point accountability is incredibly powerful, it isn't an excuse to act unilaterally. Accountability needs to be tempered with the obligation to consult and escalate issues appropriately, to ensure the best possible outcomes from any decision. Most deliverables in complex organizations require ingenuity and energy, and are difficult to achieve without a level of collaboration. The key is that it's the accountable person who drives this collaboration.

2. **It builds organizational capability.**

A strong accountability culture not only drives execution excellence, it also builds your team's capability. People grow in confidence as they become more comfortable exercising their accountabilities. They learn to take calculated risks and to make decisions without fear of being blamed for a less-than-perfect outcome. They build the strength to seek input and get opinions from others to help shape their decisions and to deliver the outcomes they're accountable for. This is how they learn and grow, but it requires a culture of excellence over perfection and a commitment to individual empowerment, which we'll look at shortly.

In previous chapters we've discussed how to become comfortable with conflict, build greater personal resilience, and master highly ambiguous situations. An accountable person who knows that they're individually charged with achieving an outcome will get the opportunity to use all of these skills. On the other hand, a person who's task-focused rather than outcome-focused may never get that same opportunity to grow. When individuals remain weak, so too does the overall capability of your organization.

3. **It enables you to work at the right level.**

A strong accountability culture lets you execute without having to micromanage. You can leave people to their own devices when they have clear accountability for outcomes, and monitor their progress without getting into the *how*. You need to give them clarity and the space to perform to the best of their ability. They need to be adult enough to communicate progress appropriately, and come to you for help if things aren't going well. We'll discuss this a little more shortly.

4. **It increases your people's job satisfaction.**

Once people can see the value of clear, single-point accountabilities, and feel the exhilaration of being empowered to make a difference, any distrust or fear they had turns to discretionary effort. The self-esteem that comes from achieving something challenging and worthwhile, from being able to make a difference, and from having a tangible impact on the environment around them will surprise even the most recalcitrant of your people.

I'll always remember Graeme, a long-standing employee at a large industrial business I ran. He'd worked in warehousing and inventory control for much of his career, and was approaching retirement. When we started to push accountability down through the organization, giving individuals empowerment to make decisions, Graeme immediately understood the benefits. He took the opportunity to change some of the processes and procedures that had long been bugbears, making them more efficient and streamlined.

When his bosses saw the difference Graeme was making, they gave him more latitude, and let him make decisions across a broader range of business outcomes. The more scope he was given, the more engaged he became, and the harder he worked.

Here's the interesting thing. Graeme was completely transformed as an individual—the resignation to his lot in life and the lack of control he'd felt for so long were replaced by a newfound optimism, motivation, and zest. His demeanor completely changed—once a stooped, slow-moving man with the world on his shoulders, he got a spring in his step that you would normally only see in a man many years his junior.

In his last few years approaching retirement, Graeme added more value to the organization than he had likely done in all his years of employment, delivering hundreds of thousands of dollars in ongoing efficiencies. He did this with the same team, the same systems, and the same supplier contracts he had previously contended with. The only difference was that he'd accepted the empowerment that came with his newly defined accountabilities, and had the courage to try a new way of working.

One word of caution, however: weak accountability cultures can be difficult to change.

Not everyone is a Graeme. If you're trying to implement a strong accountability culture where it has never existed, some of your people will be fearful and suspicious. They may think that you're trying to create scapegoats. This happens mostly in low-trust environments, which is why leadership connection is so important for your people. They need to be confident that you're not trying to catch them out but, instead, to support them to do their jobs more effectively.

If your people believe that they don't have control of their environment, the culture will be hard to change. They'll see taking individual accountability for outcomes as a backwards step. This thinking is reinforced by the urban legends about what happened to their colleagues over the years, who were punished for trying to deliver an outcome and not succeeding. *Taking accountability can be a career-limiting move, so avoid it at all costs!*

The prevailing wisdom, then, is that it's better not to try at all than to stick your head above the trenches. This becomes a cultural deadweight, and the safety-in-numbers principle proliferates. *If we all keep our heads down, we'll all be OK—they can't sack all of us, can they?!*

That's why the next piece of the accountability puzzle is so crucial. Without empowerment, accountability is just leadership cruelty, and it will reinforce your people's deepest, darkest fears. Often, when I looked at the enormity of the challenge in front of me to transform a weak accountability culture, I knew that I couldn't start there. I had to go back a step further, and start with empowerment.

When I faced several hundred blue-collar employees on my first visit to a difficult operational site, I remember the skepticism in their eyes. I embodied *change*, the one thing they were hell-bent on avoiding. But I didn't ask anything of them at that stage. Instead, I said, "You have no reason to give me the benefit of the doubt. I can say whatever I like, but that's not going to make any difference to you. Let's just have a look at where we are this time next year, and see if anything has improved. The first thing you'll notice in this change is that you'll feel you're being listened to. That's our first step, and until that happens, nothing else can."

Listening to people was a good start to get their attention, but that's just the first step on the long road to an accountability culture. So I went about working with the company's leadership, at all levels, to increase the level of empowerment each individual was given.

EMPOWERMENT: THE FLIP SIDE OF ACCOUNTABILITY

If you're going to make someone accountable for delivering an outcome, you have to give them the autonomy to do what you've asked them to do. Without empowerment, you put your accountable people in an impossible position. If you set impossible objectives, the energy and magic of single-point accountability is replaced by cynicism and demotivation.

Empowerment may seem like a simple concept, but it can't be achieved simply by following the old axiom *hire great people and then get out of their way*. It starts with the assignment of a task, and doesn't finish until the value from the deliverable is banked. Empowering your people requires a lot more than just resisting the temptation to interfere in their day-to-day work—it's a very interactive and deliberate process.

1. Clarify objectives and expectations.

Before you set objectives for any deliverable, check to make sure your people understand the context. This comes back to the communication of purpose, strategy, and tactics. Is it clear to them how the initiative fits into the bigger picture? Is it clear how this contributes to the organization's goals, and delivers value for its stakeholders?

Having incredibly clear objectives for delivery is a prerequisite for empowerment. Agreement on what outcomes will be used to measure success helps your people to know where to focus their energy and attention. And this is not just a one-time deal—it's important to give people feedback as they work through any activity, to help them calibrate their expectations with yours.

Always come back to the agreed objectives, and test progress against them. There will be many coaching opportunities on both the what and the how, as you guide your people to deliver high-quality outcomes.

2. Give them decision rights.

Letting your people make all the necessary decisions to deliver the outcomes they're accountable for is critical. If you truly want to preserve the power of single-point accountability, don't dilute it by sharing decision-making account-ability with others—this is the fastest way to weaken your execution capability.

Stepping across your people's decision rights, either explicitly or implicitly, allows them to relax. *Martin has made the call on this one, so he's going to be just as accountable as I am if it all goes to custard!* This may seem obvious, but it's not. Sometimes the influence we exert over a decision is subtle, but no less impactful.

Before I genuinely understood this principle, I fell into the trap frequently. I thought I was giving people the freedom to make their decisions, but I had my thumb on the scale. I would often say things like, "OK, this is completely your call, but if I were going to make it, I'd probably go in this direction." I had just unwittingly told them what to do.

As leaders, we sometimes forget the old adage that *what my boss finds interesting, I'm completely fascinated by.* Even the seemingly harmless act of expressing a preference for a certain decision to one of your people can dilute their decision-making accountability to the point where they lose the focus and commitment you want them to have.

3. Agree on clear delivery dates.

Stretching people to perform is a critical part of releasing their capability, and this is done most effectively by setting the right deadlines. I've separated this from setting other expectations because we all become energized around a deadline. Any deadline you set should have three defining characteristics. It should be:

- **LOGICAL**—A deadline has to have a clear reason for being where it is.

- **AMBITIOUS**—It should be challenging but achievable (otherwise it demotivates rather than energizes).

- **FLEXIBLE**—As events change, so should your preparedness to review the deadline.

Ideally, deadlines are agreed to or, even better, set by the accountable person, with your guidance. People will rally around a deadline that they've bought into, and there's no better way to achieve buy-in than by letting a person create the target themselves.

Sometimes, deadlines are mandated by external forces. Remember the Y2K problem? Companies had to prepare their technology systems to handle the transition to the year 2000. That deadline was clear and immovable: midnight on December 31, 1999. If the work wasn't completed by then, it never would be. In the end, Y2K was uneventful—so much so that some claimed it was all a hoax. But I prefer to think that the magic of an immovable deadline drove accountable people to deal with the biggest risks before they exploded.

4. Provide appropriate resources.

Setting objectives for the delivery of outcomes is only relevant if it's done in the context of available resources. There's nothing quite as soul-destroying for your people as being sent off on a fool's errand. You can't ask someone to deliver an outcome with $1 million and 10 people, when in reality it requires $5 million and 50 people.

I've seen countless examples of people being set up to fail, because the deliverables and deadlines simply couldn't be achieved with the available resources. It's true that constraining resources can bring out an untapped level of commitment and ingenuity, but if this principle is taken too far it just breeds a sense of futility.

The most efficient use of resources I ever experienced in my corporate career happened when I was CIO of a leading insurance company. We had set out to replace the core systems of the business—underwriting, claims, workflow, reporting, the whole suite—with a bespoke software development. With experience in software development projects of this type, I estimated that it would likely require between $30 million and $40 million of capital to achieve the desired outcome, if we'd followed traditional methods. Instead, the team delivered the project for less than $13 million! Because that was all the money the board was prepared to invest in a business of our size.

But there were consequences to this. We shifted the delivery date more than once. A number of people faced severe burnout, including myself. We used a lot of free, open-source software, rather than purchasing software that was backed with the comfort of a support regime from an IBM or SAP. The first release of the software was really clunky, and it took several months to stabilize the new system. It also drove our main service provider, a software development company, into severe financial distress.

In the end, it proved to be an incredibly valuable investment that underpinned our competitive advantage for years to come. But it came with a hefty price tag in terms of the human impacts. You couldn't sail any closer to the wind than we did on this one, and it set a new benchmark in my head for capital efficiency.

But don't try this at home! Whatever you do, make sure you provide sufficient people, money, and assets so that your accountable leaders don't fall into the zone of impossibility.

5. Be available to coach and mentor.

Make it easy for your people to access you, and make the experience a positive one. One of your most important roles as a leader is to *challenge*, *coach*, and *confront* your people, which we'll cover in the next chapter. The *coaching* piece requires you to be as available as necessary to provide high-quality guidance to your accountable people when they run into problems.

Your job isn't to solve their problems for them, or to conveniently provide the answers they can't arrive at themselves. It's to help them to learn how to make decisions by exposing them to the practical decision-making tools we discussed in the previous chapter. Guide them as to how much input they should seek, how much data they should analyze, and how to evaluate the risks of the options they're weighing.

At the CEO level, I spent almost half my time coaching and mentoring my executives and their accountable leaders. Every conversation brought greater understanding, and helped them to grow by allowing them to make decisions and develop their own leadership fingerprint.

If you can create a *no blame, no excuses* culture, people will come to you for guidance, and what happens in those coaching moments builds the capability your organization needs to flourish.

6. Provide support for cross-team skirmishes.

Regardless of how strongly you implement the accountability and decision-making framework in your team, there will be many people who aren't accountable but feel as though they have a contribution to make. Sometimes, they just want to give you their expert opinion, and sometimes the accountable person won't like it.

Striking a balance here can be tricky. At one company, our trading and analytics team was one of the most critical teams in the organization—that's how we sold wholesale energy into a dynamically traded market. The strategy for balancing our exposure to the spot market with long-term customer agreements and presold derivatives contracts was highly complex.

The executive accountable for trading was very knowledgeable and respected, but relatively new to the executive ranks. Two of his peers, the CFO and the chief commercial officer, were also incredibly intelligent, experienced, and gifted executives. Both of these executives had previously run similar trading desks in different organizations.

When it came to discussions about trading strategy, to say that the conversation became feisty at times would be an understatement. For me, as CEO, I couldn't have asked for better. I had three capable, passionate executives trying to wrestle highly complex and critical issues to ground. All three individuals were steadfast in the superiority of their views—often wrong, never in doubt! Occasionally, two would fall into alignment, but it was extremely rare that all three would agree on anything.

As the revenue of the organization hinged almost entirely on some of these decisions, I found myself playing referee more than once. And here's the thing—as much as I respected and trusted the non-accountable executives, my default position was to *back the accountable executive*. Why? Because he was the one who would ultimately be held to account for the results.

If the accountable executive was clearly not listening, or becoming obstinate in his position, I would quietly pull him aside and have a conversation. As I said, accountability doesn't give anyone the right to act unilaterally. But the importance of allowing the accountable person to make the decisions that impacted his ability to deliver value was the only way to energize and motivate that leader and his team to produce exceptional work—which they did!

7. **Let them succeed or fail on their merits.**

This is the part where you step back and let your people be their best. If you've done everything else to empower them, they should be able to take it from there. Of course, the feeling of being supported, not being set up as a fall guy, is the critical cultural lever that will dictate how the accountable person feels about this new level of empowerment.

My wonderful wife, Kathy, learned quickly about the relationship between accountability and empowerment. Early in our marriage, when she'd ask me to do something around the house, Kathy would often instruct me on how to deliver the job to her satisfaction. I quickly revealed the concept of accountability and empowerment.

"Darling", I said, "you have two options: you can ask me to do something, or you can do it yourself. There isn't a third option where you ask me to do something and then get to tell me how to do it. If you're happy for me to do the job, then you're going to have to be happy with the way I choose to do it. But if it's important to you that it's done a certain way, it's all yours." That was thirteen years ago, and we often laugh about this now. (And yes, we're *still* very happily married!)

Many leaders talk about empowering their people, but never take the deliberate actions that make this a reality. The better you are at genuinely empowering your people, the more likely they are to accept the accountability you give them. This is what creates execution excellence, and this is what separates the dogs from the fleas.

ACCOUNTABILITY IN COMPLEX ORGANIZATIONS

Large organizations are complex beasts. They often have multiple geographical locations, multiple products, and multiple customer segments. In an effort to meet these often competing demands, organizational structures have become equally complex. But single-point accountability is still critical in even the most complex organizations.

There are two basic philosophies for structuring organizations (and a million hybrid variations of each).

| Business Unit Structure

In organizations where business units have primacy, there's an accountable executive (often a CEO) at the head of each business unit, who's entirely accountable for the outcomes of her part of the organization. For example, a company like General Electric has business units based on industry sectors—energy, healthcare, aviation, etc.

The business unit head would control all resources to deliver that product, from design and engineering through to sales. They would also work out how much support they needed for corporate services like HR, IT, and legal.

These organizations typically have a very lean head office, which handles group-wide financial reporting, corporate strategy, investor relations, capital allocation, etc.

Business unit structures promote extremely high accountability. There's clearly one head to pat, and one arse to kick—the executive accountable for that business unit. This gives them a huge amount of autonomy, and promotes lean support structures. When an executive is held to account for the profit and loss (P&L), it really makes them think hard about every dollar they spend in non-revenue-generating services. This drives a high level of individual performance in the business units.

On the downside, an organization structured along business unit lines gets little benefit from overall economies of scale and scope. There's often a lack of consistency between business units, and there's almost no sharing of ideas, methods, and talent. Collaboration is very difficult to promote in an every-unit-for-itself culture.

| Functional Structure

In organizations that are structured along functional lines, the products and services would all fall under the purview of an executive accountable for that function. These are sometimes called *matrix* structures. For example, there may be a chief operating officer who's accountable for all operations, cutting across multiple markets, geographies, and product segments. The head of commercial and marketing would be accountable for the design, marketing, and sales of *all* products across a broad portfolio.

This type of structure often creates confusion as to who's accountable for what—where does the job of operations end and marketing begin? Although functional structures may lack the extreme clarity that comes from business unit structures, they too have their advantages.

Functional structures tend to create a high level of consistency between divisions. Collaboration is easier to embed, and synergies between the various divisions are easier to identify and capitalize on. Talent management is enhanced, facilitating the movement of high-potential people between divisions in order to provide the right development opportunities.

Functional structures also achieve economies of scale through greater centralization of resources. For example, aggregating demand for a supply contract in almost any area allows you to negotiate a more favorable deal—it's a very different proposition going to market for the supply of 10 widgets per month than when you're trying to source 100,000 widgets per month.

The downside is that with weaker accountability, the focus on value creation can be lost. Functional divisions that don't produce or sell products and services can become fat and happy, and these expanding divisions create a new and inefficient cost base.

| Which Structure Is Better?

First of all, it's important to realize that *any* structure works self-evidently. Organizations go through cycles of restructuring from business units, to functional models, back to business units. It really has little impact on the performance of the organization, and any benefit you think might be derived from a restructure is quickly swallowed up by the cost and ongoing disruption of implementing it.

I prefer the functional structure, only because I think it's more likely to strike the right balance between short-term and long-term value. Business unit structures tend to promote short-termism, as executives are held to account for their annual (or monthly) P&L.

The important thing is that, regardless of the structure, you must implement a strong, single-point accountability model.

Accountability in Matrix Organizations

Whether structured by business units or functions, leaders in most large organizations have multiple reporting lines. A financial controller working for the retail division of a large conglomerate might have a hard reporting line to the business unit head, but also a secondary (or dotted, or soft) reporting line to the corporate CFO.

Working out who's cooking the chook is sometimes difficult, and shared accountabilities tend to creep in. Gaps, overlaps, and inefficiencies emerge, weakening execution.

Many leaders believe that they can only be held accountable for things that they have direct and complete control over. In other words, they have to own *all* the people, *all* the money, and *all* the authority of their position, if they're to own the outcomes. This is a reinforcement of the command-and-control management philosophy, which works from the basis of positional power, not influence.

There are two problems with this misconception. The first is that in today's complex organizations, there's very little of significance that's achieved without cooperation and collaboration between different business units and functional teams. The second is that the only point at which many initiatives stream to one individual is at the CEO level—and the last thing you want is for every decision in the organization to flow up to the CEO's office.

The principle that someone can be accountable for things they don't have complete control over is fundamental to execution excellence.

The strategic decisions made by the energy market trading team (which I mentioned above) were a perfect example of having an accountable executive who didn't control all the resources. The trading team required input from the modelers in the finance team, who worked for the CFO. They had to receive approval for their trading strategies from the market risk team, which also reported to the CFO. In formulating customer proposals, they had to consult the commercial team. The CIO was accountable for delivering the software that drove the trading and risk modeling systems, and there were supporting functions like legal and HR.

But there was one head to pat, and one arse to kick—executive general manager, Energy Markets.

To get the right outcomes, he had to negotiate the deployment of resources with each of the other executives. He had to monitor the progress of the other teams' deadlines. He had to influence his peers to get the required outcomes that he was accountable for producing.

In situations where an impasse couldn't be resolved, his recourse was to me. As the ultimate escalation point, I could break up any logjams that formed between the divisions, when their priorities weren't aligned. My job was to give them the gift of clarity. In this way, exercising full accountability across multiple reporting lines breeds leaders who learn to get results through influence, not force.

| Staff vs. Line Roles

The classification of these fundamental role types was originally coined by the military, but is often used in business. A *line role* refers to any job that's focused on the core deliverables of the organization: operations, manufacturing, maintenance, sales, etc. A *staff role* is not engaged in the core activities, but is nevertheless critical to create maximum value for the business: HR, risk, IT, legal, etc.

I've seen a lot of confusion over the years when people don't properly understand the role they're meant to play. The whole concept is rather poorly understood.

When it comes to results and leadership, accountability *always* resides with the line leader. Functional leaders provide expertise, guidance, resources, and tools to support the line leader, but they don't have accountability for delivery, except as it relates to their own field. The CIO might be accountable for the delivery of the eCommerce and telecommunications infrastructure that the company uses to do its business, but not for the sales that are conducted over the eCommerce platform they provide.

Likewise, the general manager of a mine site is accountable for the safety of her people when they come to work. She is the line leader who establishes standards, sets priorities, monitors progress, makes decisions on productivity, and determines the culture of her team.

A safety manager might also be assigned to that mine site. But he *cannot* ensure the safety of the workers. He can provide input and resources; he can provide expertise on how to manage safety risks; he can help the line leader to set the right lead indicators; he can monitor the safety performance of the team; he can provide independent assessment and reporting of progress for senior management. What he *can't* do is keep the people working on that site safe—that's the job of the line leadership.

The temptation, though, is that when someone has the word "safety" in their title, the line leader can tend to feel as though *that* person is accountable for safety, which dilutes line accountability. This is an incredibly dangerous trap to fall into. Clearly defining the delineation between line and staff roles helps to avoid the confusion and uncertainty that often develops, even with the best people and the best intent.

There were many occasions in the course of my career when I had to correct leaders who didn't understand their accountabilities. On one occasion, an operational leadership team was presenting a quarterly performance review to the top team. At one point in the presentation, Trevor, the line executive, said, "Now I'll just hand it over to Robyn to talk about our succession planning." Robyn was, of course, the company's chief HR officer.

As she launched into her portion of the presentation, I interrupted and asked Trevor why Robyn was presenting. "Because she's accountable for HR"—the obvious answer. I had to explain that just because Robyn had been providing expertise to the operations team didn't mean she was accountable. Trevor owned talent and succession planning for his group, not Robyn. It was his job to grow and develop the people who had been identified as high-potential (with HR's help, of course).

Who was managing the development of talent under that scenario? *No one!* Trevor thought Robyn was, and Robyn thought Trevor was. Right under their noses, shared accountability created *no* accountability. And neither of them could see this problem.

If you want the benefit of strong accountabilities, it's important that you understand precisely what you're looking for from each type of role, and that you can explain it clearly to those involved:

LINE LEADERS

1. You own it... it's yours... make it happen!

2. We'll provide you with some expert guidance in areas where you may not have the capability (e.g., risk management).

3. We'll also set some ground rules and standards for you to observe, for the sake of organizational efficiency and consistency.

4. Here are the people you can draw upon for that support—they're here to help you.

STAFF LEADERS

- Don't get too carried away—the line leaders are accountable for delivery.

- You are the philosophical custodian of your function on behalf of the organization.

- Your job is to provide expertise, processes, and systems that add value.

- You need to listen to the line leaders to understand what drives the greatest value for them.

- You don't control the line leaders, but you must positively influence them.

- If line leaders choose not to follow the functional standards, you need to escalate.

- You're operating the scoreboard—make it clear to the line leaders what they need to do to make the scoreboard tick over, and if they're not scoring you need to let their boss know.

A strong, single-point accountability culture often eludes leaders because of the complexity of the organizational structures they have to operate within. Resolving this requires focus and dozens of conversations with the people involved to ensure they understand what they're accountable to achieve.

EAT YOUR OWN DOG FOOD

You've probably worked out that, as a leader, your people watch you pretty closely. Accountability is the one behavior that they can readily observe—and this tells them whether or not they can trust you. It also sets the standard for their own behavior.

Are you the leader who readily accepts accountability, or the leader who makes excuses and shifts blame onto everyone but yourself? If you want your people to be accountable, you have to eat your own dog food. You must be the *most* accountable person in your organization. Great leaders accept the accountability that comes with their role, and they embrace it. You can hear it in their language and see it in their approach to every problem they face.

Strong leaders hold their people to account for doing their jobs—and if they're not doing their jobs, strong leaders don't take the easy way out by micromanaging or over-functioning for their underperforming people. They try to lift their performance with the tools of empowerment, which are designed to support their success.

When one of your people isn't performing, you only have two options. The first is to trust the accountable person and support them to do their job. But if you don't trust them to do their job, you can always choose the second option: get a new accountable person whom you *do* trust! Micromanaging isn't an option—it's the default position of a weak leader.

Strong leaders create a culture of accountability that starts and stops at their desk.

CUTTING THROUGH THE BULLSH!T

Strong accountability is the key to successful execution, and if you implement nothing else from this book, driving accountability into your team will radically improve the results your people deliver.

For each of the following questions, rate yourself (on a scale of 1 to 10) before you move on to the next chapter. This will give you greater insight into what stands between you and your ability to achieve execution excellence.

1. How clear are you on who's accountable for outcomes right now?

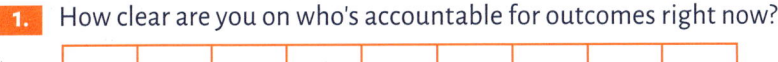

2. How comfortable are you with taking on accountability when you don't have complete control?

3. To what extent does your organization tolerate shared accountability?

4. How well do you think you empower your people to do their jobs?

5. How much would your people trust you, if you were to implement stronger accountabilities?

6. To what extent does your organization do each of the following?

• Set realistic objectives

1	2	3	4	5	6	7	8	9	10

• Resource people and initiatives appropriately

1	2	3	4	5	6	7	8	9	10

• Increase workload without providing additional resourcing

1	2	3	4	5	6	7	8	9	10

7. How likely are you to intervene in your people's decisions, and dilute their accountabilities?

1	2	3	4	5	6	7	8	9	10

8. How positive a role model are you for taking accountability?

1	2	3	4	5	6	7	8	9	10

CHAPTER 9

CONNECTING THE DOTS

THE BULLSH!T WE BELIEVE

If you were brought up in a privileged country like the USA, with a backdrop of peace, prosperity, and access to education, it's likely you were told that success comes to those who work harder than the next person. This is the promise of democratic societies, based upon individual determination and opportunity. It sounds like it should be true, because that would be *fair.* But waiting for life to be fair won't bring rewards.

I've seen countless people throughout my career who are incredibly hard workers, who are educated and smart enough to achieve anything they set their minds to, who don't reap the success that you might expect. There's a range of reasons for this, of course, but one of the most common is that they never learn how to become strong leaders. They spend too much of their career working too hard on too many of the wrong things.

Working hard is a given for anyone who wants to be successful. But choosing to work hard on the *right* things is surprisingly uncommon. The choice to become a professional leader is central to achieving career success, whether you're running a multibillion-dollar corporation or a micro start-up. Leadership starts with your habits, behaviors, and capabilities—it's only from that base that you earn the right to influence others. Ultimately, to be successful, you have to work hard *and* work smart.

We've looked at the practical fundamentals of strong leadership through the lens of the seven NO BULLSH!T LEADERSHIP imperatives. The final step in bringing this all together is to incorporate these disciplines into your day-to-day leadership work. This chapter shows how to do this, so that you can work smarter by applying your energy and discipline to the things that truly get results.

As a no bullshit leader, you'll be able to create untold value for your organization and your people, which ultimately leads to the rewards your parents and teachers told you were yours for the taking. //

TAKING DELIBERATE ACTION

I said earlier in the book that nothing happens unless a leader makes it happen, but that isn't entirely true. Lots of things happen simply because they're part of the rusted-on activity that the organization has historically undertaken. A more accurate way of describing this principle is that nothing *different* happens unless a leader makes it happen.

If you aspire to be a great leader, you need to embed great habits. There's no magic formula—it's your habits, your attitude, and the cumulative effect of every decision you've ever made that's brought you to where you are today. Want to go somewhere different? Then it's your habits, attitude, and decisions that have to change.

You need to put some structure and discipline in place to hold yourself accountable for developing as a leader: discipline that pushes you to do the *right* things, not repeat unhelpful patterns. One of the most practical ways of doing this is to create a structure of meetings that forces you to confront the things you might otherwise avoid.

These range from regular one-on-one meetings to group meetings that scrutinize team performance and value delivery. Over the years, I formulated a structured meeting cadence that was the backbone of all my leadership work, and that drove organizational performance.

The Meeting Tempo

You won't find many people working in large businesses who feel as though they'd like to attend more meetings. But meetings provide the platform for you to clearly communicate the purpose, strategy, and objectives of the organization. Meetings create the opportunity for you to connect people's individual work assignments to the organization's value drivers, showing them how they're contributing to its overall success. And meetings lay the groundwork for the hundreds of informal conversations that you'll hold with your people outside that meeting room.

To make them valuable, every meeting you schedule has to have an agenda and a purpose that's clear to everyone involved. Done intelligently, this can reduce both the number of meetings and the number of attendees in each meeting, while getting a greater return on investment for the time you spend.

One-on-One Meetings

I discovered the optimum way to schedule formal meetings with each of my direct reports. Held for an hour each fortnight, one meeting would be on *their* agenda—whatever was important to them, or that they wanted to seek my guidance on. The alternate meeting was on *my* agenda, and focused specifically on performance—both theirs and their team's. These conversations were always held with reference to very clear and well-established performance standards. It was here that much of the conflict in the individual relationships with my direct reports was drawn out and managed.

These types of meetings provide both teaching and learning opportunities. They let you build your own leadership capability, while also strengthening the relationships with your people.

One-on-one meetings are the primary means of laying the groundwork for the leadership dialogue. I found that they gave me the footing to pull any of my people aside at any point to give them specific and targeted feedback: *Hey, I noticed you changed your approach to the way you asked questions in the board meeting. That's exactly what I meant when I raised this last week in our one-on-one—great work!* Or, *We spoke last week about Greg's performance. I was just wondering if you've made the time to give him feedback yet.*

If regular meetings are scheduled with a specific agenda, you'll be less inclined to skip or postpone them. Once in the room, it's hard to avoid the very conversation that the meeting was convened to have.

In addition to the one-on-one meetings with my direct reports, I also held formal meetings with leaders at lower levels. Whilst less frequent, I met individually with everyone on the broader leadership team (50-odd leaders) twice per year.

And, most importantly, my door was always open to ensure I was available to support the leaders who needed it. This combination of meetings, both formal and informal, gave me incredible visibility into the performance and behavior of my top-level leaders and, consequently, the ability to make better decisions in regard to capability building and talent management.

Group Meetings

I held a range of group meetings on a regular basis to communicate intent, expectations, and standards.

For my executive leadership team, weekly operational meetings provided the opportunity for everyone to contribute to cross-border issues, and to align their portfolios with the corporate priorities. These meetings provoked a lot of robust discussion, and they provided great opportunities to reinforce our focus on the few key value drivers of the business.

Once a month, instead of the weekly operational meeting, we held a longer meeting with a more strategic agenda. This meeting gave us half a day to analyze the performance of the business in some detail, and to make any decisions necessary to optimize for the coming month and beyond.

Each quarter, I would bring the broader management team together for two days to communicate and discuss the organization's priorities. These forums included quarterly business reviews, where each executive in turn would bring *their* leadership teams to the table to present a detailed analysis of last quarter's results, and to give their prognosis for the next quarter and full year. This was a tremendous forum for holding leaders to account for doing what they said they'd do, and ensuring the focus on delivering value was unequivocal.

And, finally, annual planning sessions were critical in determining how to best invest the company's resources in order to create the most value. This was our first, best bet for eradicating the low-value work that seems to get a life of its own in most organizations.

| Changing Your Own Leadership Habits

The meeting cadence will give you the footing to engage with your people in a meaningful way—it's a vehicle for you to exercise strong leadership. We'll look at the key elements of this shortly—setting the *tone*, the *pace*, and the *standard* for your team, and using the *challenge, coach, confront* framework to manage individual performance.

Beyond this, you need to develop different habits to change the way you lead. You need to hold yourself to account for doing things differently. There are many tools in the preceding chapters that will help you to hold yourself to account. For example:

- If you make a habit of focusing on other people rather than yourself, and using the five lenses of the psychology of feedback, you'll find it much easier to deliver difficult messages when required.

- If you use the decision-tracking questions to hold yourself to account for the speed of your decision-making, you'll inevitably become more decisive.

- If you use the perspective questions when a crisis is brewing, you'll eventually become better equipped to deal with crises.

- If you use the guidelines for communicating to your people in times of ambiguity, you'll create clarity for them, and for you.

- If you use the technique of replacing your anger and frustration with curiosity, you'll stay calmer and more controlled during negotiations.

These are just a few of the tools from previous chapters that you can now take forward to improve your leadership habits. But remember, we all have blind spots, and there's nothing like a trusted advisor who's prepared to tell you the brutal truth to keep you grounded.

SETTING THE TONE, PACE, AND STANDARD

A friend at a dinner party once asked me what I did. When I told her that I was CEO of an energy business, she said, "Yes, I know that, but what do you actually do?"

I fumbled around for a while, giving examples of all the things that filled my days, trying not to use too many words that would qualify for a game of bullshit bingo. But I'm not sure that she was any the wiser at the end of our conversation.

I mulled this over for a few days before I landed on the right description. As CEO, I set the *tone*, the *pace*, and the *standard* for the company. This is done through every interaction, formal and informal, written and verbal, and it should be the case for any leader of leaders who has stewardship of their organization's resources.

Tone

Tone is about behavioral and cultural norms. It lets people know what's OK and what's not OK, and it sets the parameters of your expectations. Regardless of what's happening next to you or above you in your organization, you have an obligation as a leader to set the tone for *your* team.

Start by setting the positive tone—your expectations for every individual to display personal integrity, be accountable for outcomes, and deliver value. All of these cues come from the leader and need to be continually reinforced.

But every organization develops bad habits over time, and what becomes acceptable is sometimes well beyond the limits of normal conduct.

I had a zero-tolerance policy for unethical, deceptive, or self-seeking behavior, and the leaders who worked for me knew it. I've been in more than one organization where I've had to explicitly tell people that certain norms that had crept into the culture over time were completely unacceptable, and wouldn't be tolerated.

One of these was the entrenched practice of teams scheduling their sick leave to maximize the pay packets of each team member. If one person called in sick, and another had to be contacted at short notice to work on their day off, this would attract penalty payments. The individual working un-rostered shift hours was rewarded with twice the normal pay rate.

I couldn't have been more direct on this issue. Although some workers might have seen this practice as an acceptable way to reap the entitlements in their cushy employment agreement, it wasn't. It was *theft*, and it wouldn't be tolerated. I told them in no uncertain terms that any instances of this behavior that we uncovered would result in the summary dismissal of the individual. I doubt that the practice stopped entirely, but it certainly made a few people think, particularly the front-line supervisors who were allowing this to go on under their noses.

| Pace

People will always be happy to go slower than they could. Even your best people like targets to be readily achievable, and tend to set deadlines that are less challenging than they're capable of meeting. To break this habit, you need to bring a sense of urgency to everything your people do.

For me, everything happened too slowly, so I set unreasonable expectations for the pace the organization moved at. The opportunity cost of doing things different-ly—safer, faster, and more efficiently—drove me onward. Every day that we weren't improving, we were getting further behind the performance benchmarks we were chasing. Every day that we didn't improve our safety cul-ture brought us a day closer to one of our people having a serious injury.

This weighed heavily on me as CEO, and I had to be careful not to allow my drive for pace to turn into frustra-tion. Many people thought we were already moving too quickly. But when our productivity benchmarks showed that we needed to improve by more than 80 percent in some areas to reach top-quartile performance, that was a huge worry.

Saying "go faster" isn't that helpful, though, unless you show your people *how* to go faster. We invested a significant amount of money into operational productivity improve-ments, and hired top consulting firms to help us develop a robust methodology for improvement.

We also showed that, through faster decision-making, we could get better results more quickly. Strong single-point accountabilities, a culture of excellence over perfection, and commitment to the deadlines we set were all crucial elements.

In one instance, while managing a legal dispute with one of our suppliers, our chief lawyer told the board that it would take two months before we'd be in a position to commence litigation. Given the deterioration of the current relationship, there was no way we could wait that long, so I pushed the legal team to take a different ap-proach to their preparation.

We didn't need every duck perfectly lined up—what we needed was a strong, timely shot over the bow of the supplier. But getting the legal team to set aside their customary conservatism and take a riskier approach was extraordinarily difficult. Constant energy is needed to increase your organization's pace.

| Standard

The standard you walk past is the standard you set. If you aren't constantly reinforcing the high standards you're trying to achieve, you're giving tacit approval to whatever's happening within your team, regardless of whether or not you agree with it.

That's why diligent performance review and talent management regimes are so important. It's through these processes that you communicate the baseline for acceptable performance. The standard for your team's performance isn't set by your best performer, it's set by your *weakest* performer. That's the person on the team whom your good people look at and say, "Well, if Jerry can perform that poorly and still keep his job, I guess that must be the acceptable performance standard."

Taking a deliberate approach to defining and communicating the performance standard is the first step and, as a leader, you need to ensure that people rise to the minimum acceptable standard. It has to be underpinned by an up-or-out mentality: *We'd love you all to be wildly successful, so we're setting very clear standards for you to meet. This way, you know what our expectations are, and you can choose whether you're prepared to meet these expectations.*

To properly set the tone, the pace, and the standard, you need to be strong enough to handle conflict comfortably, and to work at the right level. You need to be resilient when the inertia of the organization feels overwhelming, and you need to hold people to account for their individual performance and behavior. People need to step into the vacuum you leave when you refuse to work below your level. If you adopt the NO BULLSH!T LEADERSHIP philosophy, it's much more likely that you'll do this successfully.

CHALLENGE, COACH, CONFRONT

Strong leaders master the skill of *challenging*, *coaching*, and *confronting* their people. This is the process through which the seven imperatives of NO BULLSH!T LEADERSHIP are brought to life for your people. Every interaction you have with them is an opportunity for you to either enhance or hamper their performance, behavior, and results, and your regular meeting cadence provides frequent opportunities for this.

In a constructive, high-performance culture, you need to be able to clearly and rapidly set expectations, and then manage them effectively. Competent application of the challenge, coach, confront framework can have a huge impact on individual and team performance.

At its simplest level, people want to know three things when they come to work each day:

1. What are your expectations of me?

2. How am I performing in relation to those expectations?

3. What does my future hold?

Can your people answer these questions? It would surprise me greatly if they could—I've tested this over and over during keynote speeches by asking for a show of hands of who thinks their people know the answer to these three questions with a fair degree of certainty. The response rate is usually around 5 percent, and never greater than 10 percent. If you think about this from your own perspective, how often during your career have those answers been obvious to you? I've worked for some excellent bosses who didn't give me any real clarity, but fortunately, I was strong enough to keep pushing forward without it. Most people aren't.

Challenging, coaching, and confronting are at the heart of the leadership dialogue. It goes on every day in interactions, big and small, formal and informal, verbal and written. It gives people the context they can confidently operate within, which in turn enables them to make good decisions without continually second-guessing themselves.

It's through this framework that trust is built and culture is established. If you do this properly, you'll spend 95 percent of your time in the first two phases (challenging and coaching), and very little time confronting. If you find yourself spending more than 5 percent of your time confronting an individual, this is a red flag. It means either that you're not challenging and coaching well enough, or that you've let someone slip into chronic underperformance.

Either way, you should be looking to change that situation so that you can spend the majority of your time with your best people—those who create the most value for your organization. Challenging, coaching, and confronting can take place at both the individual and group level, as long as you observe the basic tenets of decency and respect. For example, don't confront an individual in a group setting—it's disrespectful, and it kills trust.

Let's take a look at the three parts of the model in more detail.

| Challenge

This is the starting point, where you make your expectations clear to an accountable individual, and seek agreement and commitment to meeting those expectations. It's the basis for clarifying everything from the organizational values, through to the performance standards, behavioral norms, and cultural expectations.

This is where you articulate the tone, pace, and standard that you're setting, and have conversations about what that means to the individual in their specific role. It's also the best opportunity for you to reinforce the approaches that you're trying to embed in your culture.

The most common issue I see with leaders in this phase is that they're afraid to really stretch their people. This is about setting the expectation for individuals to be their best. It's not about asking unreasonable things of them, nor is it simply a proxy for burying them under an oppressive workload.

Even your very best performers won't stretch themselves beyond about 80 percent of their existing capability without you driving them to do so.

You may feel uncomfortable about the amount of stress you put your people under, and may be unwilling to ask them to do difficult things. If you're giving them the *right* work—only those things that add *real* value, not just fill their days with inane or ineffective activity—you'll find that people have much more capacity than you might have imagined.

The word *stress* generally carries negative connotations, but stress isn't necessarily bad. Work done over a century ago by two American psychologists resulted in the creation of their eponymous Yerkes–Dodson law, which explains the relationship between stress and performance. This law shows that stress is an important ingredient for superior performance. Increasing stress actually *improves* performance, up to a point. But once that point is reached, performance declines when more stress is added.

As a leader, it's important to understand where each person's limits are—everyone is different. Your job is to help them stretch to that optimum point, and if you can manage to go just a fraction beyond it, you'll see someone move into *flow* state, where performance transcends what even they thought was possible.

In his book *The Rise of Superman*, Steven Kotler discusses the application of the Yerkes–Dodson law for extreme athletes. The desire and ability to stretch just a fraction beyond the limit of their capabilities is what creates the magic. Pushing your people into a heightened state of positive stress is what releases their resourcefulness and energy, creating the environment for them to perform at their best. Don't be afraid to give your people this gift—they'll thank you for it!

Trying to keep people happy is not necessarily in their best interests. One of our podcast listeners with a background in the military described it this way: "Soldiers with high morale aren't 'happy'; they are confident, secure, and enabled to perform. They're not well-fed, rested, and kept out of harm's way."

| Coach

This is the fun part of leadership. After setting the right objectives, and ensuring that your accountable person is well-resourced, coaching provides the opportunity for you to guide and support them.

Coaching enables you gain a clear understanding of the issues your people face, and to guide them through their decision-making processes. It lets you see their fears and apprehension, and to identify their limiting beliefs and potential derailers. It opens the door for you to reinforce the messages that give them extreme clarity on your expectations.

And, yes, it provides the forum for you to deliver the occasional hard message. If you've stretched people adequately in the goal-setting phase when you challenge them, you'll keep toggling between coaching and challenging, always feeling for that optimum point of stress that releases their best performance.

Do you think any of this would be possible without a high level of emotional intelligence? Without the ability to handle conflict? Or to sit comfortably in ambiguity? And how can you coach properly if you can't work at the right level? People don't necessarily want you to do their work for them, but they do want you to build scaffolding around them to provide essential support. This is what the NO BULLSH!T LEADERSHIP tools are designed to do.

Coaching is the perfect forum for delivering difficult but crucial feedback to help people with their long-term career planning and development, answering that question, *What does my future hold?* Several years ago, I was coaching Bianca, a high-potential leader who, unfortunately, had an aversion to taking advice and guidance, particularly from people whom she wanted to impress with her vast knowledge.

Whilst Bianca was performing reasonably well in her current role, I could see clearly the way this flaw would derail her future career aspirations. I used the leadership coaching process to give her very specific and unequivocal feedback. I said, "Until you work out how to get this behavior under control and manage it effectively, you won't go any further—it's a career killer. It's limiting your obvious potential in so many ways. But because it's a deep-seated part of your psyche, I can't help you with the solution. Unfortunately, nothing will change until you decide to change it. How long will that take? Anywhere between a week and...forever. It's entirely up to you, and you may never make the choice to put in the effort and attention you need to sort it out. But now, at least you know the choices you're facing."

| Confront

Believe it or not, that conversation with Bianca wasn't part of the confront phase. That was a positive conversation to help her calibrate her future expectations with her current behaviors, giving her an opportunity to reflect and respond.

Confronting happens when people are unresponsive to the challenge and coach phases. This is the tough bit that most leaders prefer to avoid—and avoidance comes in a couple of forms. Most commonly, leaders avoid confrontation by ignoring the problem. They hope that either no one will notice, or that the problem will magically go away of its own accord. But I've also seen leaders contriving bullshit excuses to exit someone from an organization without any feedback or due process—think mini-restructures. This type of avoidance is cowardly, and it's HR's worst nightmare, but it's a surprisingly common ploy for weak leaders.

Confronting happens when someone is clearly not meeting the expectations that you've agreed on in the challenge and coach phases, either because they're unwilling or incapable of doing so. Incapable is the hardest, because that requires you to explain how they ended up in a job that they aren't suitable for. It's not always well received.

But if you've worked out that someone is unwilling to perform, that's a much easier conversation. If you can see that they have the capability but choose not to take your feedback on board, preferring to do things their own way and repeatedly failing, that can only go on for so long before they're held to account.

That's why, often, confronting someone can shift the balance of power that you deploy from influencing to controlling—there are occasions when you need to be quite directive. In Chapter 5, we looked briefly at the power of influence, referent power, as the optimum way to get results, particularly as you transition to higher levels of leadership. The power of influence is always preferred, but if someone isn't responding to this, you'll have to shift to using other forms of power. Sometimes, when people are faced with the impending reality of being dismissed from their role, the power of coercion can unlock their desire.

People need to be given difficult feedback, particularly when the potential consequences for them are as severe as being exited from the organization. Your obligation is to get that message across in the most vivid way possible, even if it means calling on some of the cruder forms of power.

It's important, though, that a confronting conversation is fair, and that the individual experiences it that way. If you've challenged and coached them competently, that will almost always be the case. Remember, if your people trust and respect you, there's *nothing* you can't say to them. Challenging and coaching are your opportunities to build that trust and respect.

If you haven't challenged and coached well, confronting will potentially be seen as unfair, and this can have devastating effects on the culture of your organization.

You can't competently deploy the challenge, coach, confront framework unless you've built the fundamentals of your leadership repertoire:

- An unshakable belief in the tenet of respect before popularity

- The acknowledgement of people's right to make their own choices about how they perform and behave

- A commitment to your duty of care, ensuring everyone has the feedback they need to make their choices wisely

- A burning desire to put the good of your people and the team ahead of your own narrow self-interest

- The skill and drive to interact with people in the most difficult and uncomfortable of circumstances

No bullshit leaders master this framework, and everyone around them reaps the benefits.

HIGH-PERFORMING TEAMS

How many times have you heard someone claim to have built a high-performing team? It's almost a given these days that it will appear on every senior leader's résumé. But most of it's just spin. Not many people can clearly articulate what a high-performing team is, let alone systematically build one.

During a corporate career in which I spent decades trying to build high-performing teams, I succeeded once (for certain), and maybe on one other occasion (at a pinch). It's not easy.

High-performing teams start with high-performing individuals—there are no tourists! Every individual has to be strong in their own right before the ingredients of the team can be brought together. And it's at this first hurdle that most fall. Weak leaders tolerate poor performers and convince themselves that everyone is performing adequately. Any objective measure would quickly dispel this rationalization.

The talent you've got isn't necessarily the talent you need. That's why it's vital to continuously improve the organization's bench strength and build the leadership capability of the future. This runs through all aspects of the life cycle, from recruitment and selection, to managing performance, developing individuals, and exiting those who choose not to meet the standard you set.

You can't claim to have built a high-performing team unless you've systematically developed the individual leadership talent that would make it true. But it's a lot easier to just believe your own bullshit. Rationalization is a comfortable cocoon for a weak leader, and there's always a battery of excuses.

Building a high-performing team requires you to be completely comfortable with conflict, to be able to make great decisions quickly, and to create clear lines of accountability that put the hot lights of performance on the individual. Sitting around telling your people how awesome they are doesn't turn them into a high-performing team—on the contrary, it weakens their capability and distorts their perspective.

In one role, I had five executives reporting directly to me. Over the course of my tenure, I replaced nine of them—that's almost two people changed out in every position. Two of these individuals were excellent performers who went on to bigger and better things. But seven left at my suggestion, as they simply weren't able to do their job to the standard I needed. Clearly, my judgment in hiring wasn't exemplary!

But these executives weren't all obvious underperformers. I just knew they weren't capable of taking their part of the business to where it needed to be. If I let them remain in their roles, I wouldn't necessarily have attracted the ire of the board, and most of the people in the company wouldn't have known any different. But *I* knew! And I couldn't let inferior performance get in the way of making the organization the best it could possibly be. They were hard calls to make, but they had to be made.

There are many teams in the world of professional sports that demonstrate what it takes to achieve high performance. Michael Jordan and Phil Jackson's Chicago Bulls won six NBA championships between 1991 and 1998. Tom Brady and Bill Belichick's New England Patriots won six Super Bowl championships from nine appearances in 18 years. In a game where this isn't supposed to be possible, every other year for almost two decades, the Patriots were the best team in the AFC!

Performance like this isn't accidental. Once you've set the standard for individual performance, you can look to the team as a whole. Although there are many characteristics of high-performing teams, I like to consider seven key indicators.

1. They get results.

2. They stand out from other teams and organizations.

3. They're never happy with the status quo.

4. They compare favorably to the scrutiny of global benchmarking.

5. They constantly challenge themselves to be better.

6. They exude confidence, because they're used to winning.

7. They don't make excuses, and they relish the toughest challenges.

Clearly, it's difficult to drive this level of performance, and it's not until you have the right personnel that you can aspire to build the right team. If you aren't prepared to do the work required to build a high-performing team, that's OK. Just don't kid yourself that you've done it if you haven't. Unless you're actively and continually working on team capability and performance, your team will be average to mediocre, so don't believe your own bullshit.

BUILDING A NO BULLSHIT CULTURE

Over time, what you focus on will determine the culture of your team. As you set the tone, the pace, and the standard with energy and conviction, you'll attract more of the right types of people, and you'll retain them. Those who don't feel they fit will eventually self-select and move to a less demanding role in another organization.

To bring the culture to life, the way you communicate is all-important. People rally around the language that describes their shared values, because it quickly evokes a positive image in their mind's eye.

There's an emerging body of work in the field of marketing on *brand language*. Many brands link words to their companies in the hope that customers will adopt and associate that language with the experience that the brand creates. Company taglines often draw this link.

- *The world is ours*—Discovery Channel

- *Just do it*—Nike

- *Think different*—Apple

These types of connections are incredibly powerful, but some companies manage to go even further, associating common-use words with their brand without using slogans or taglines. If I asked you what comes before the word *Princess*, chances are you would come up with *Disney*. Using the words *big* and *blue* next to each other may immediately conjure up IBM.

Some brands, like Starbucks, even create their own unique lexicon in order to bind their customers to them more closely. What on earth is a Trenta? Apparently, it's the largest size of cup available at Starbucks, holding 31 ounces of liquid. This nomenclature is specific to that brand, and Starbucks clearly believes that using unique terminology will build brand identification and loyalty in the customer base.

We can learn a lot from brand language that can be applied to help us embed the NO BULLSH!T LEADERSHIP principles. Culture is about what you do, how you behave, and what you show your people is important. If you reward long hours and hard work, that's what you'll get. If you reward the outcomes that create value for the organization, that's what you'll get. In this way, developing a common language as a rallying cry and focal point for your people will accelerate any culture change you implement.

Think of the cues you can give your people to help them focus on what's important. Once you show them what you want, you need to give them the language to describe it. Short phrases that evoke immediate understanding are invaluable, for example:

- **RESPECT BEFORE POPULARITY**—Do what's right, not what's popular.

- **VALUE OVER ACTIVITY**—We don't do anything just for the sake of doing it—everything must lead to a clear value outcome.

- **EXCELLENCE OVER PERFECTION**—That's good enough— don't get stuck on it. Keep moving.

- **ONE HEAD TO PAT, ONE ARSE TO KICK**—Who is individually accountable for delivering this outcome?

- **IT'S A LOT EASIER TO REIN IN A STALLION THAN IT IS TO FLOG A DONKEY**—Instead of wasting your energy on someone who's never going to get there, make the tough decision and move on.

- **THE STANDARD YOU WALK PAST IS THE STANDARD YOU SET**—If you're not committed to holding people to account for meeting the minimum required standard, who is?

- **DON'T DIP DOWN**—Work at the level you're supposed to, and hold your people to account for working at theirs.

- **IF YOU THINK THE SAME AS ME THEN AT LEAST ONE OF US IS REDUNDANT (AND IT PROBABLY ISN'T ME)**—Don't just tell me what I already know—bring something unique and valuable to the conversation.

I'm sure you've found many phrases in this book that you can use to build the language of your culture. What's the most important thing to you, and how do you encapsulate it in words that everyone can identify with? You may have phrases of your own that are more relevant to your context, but whatever you do, make sure that the language you use helps people to get a clear picture of the culture you're trying to create.

Bringing the imperatives of NO BULLSH!T LEADERSHIP to life happens through the everyday interactions with your people, as you set high standards and help them to achieve them. Superior performance, and the exceptional results that this creates, starts a virtuous circle that builds a winning team.

CUTTING THROUGH THE BULLSH!T

You'll only become a better leader by deliberately and consistently doing things differently. This book provides the practical system that will reliably improve your capability, confidence, and results. What you need to do now is to work out how to apply it in your context.

For each of the following questions, rate yourself (on a scale of 1 to 10) before you move on to the book's conclusion. This will give you greater insight into what stands between you and your ultimate goal of becoming a genuine no bullshit leader.

1. To what extent does your current meeting cadence facilitate leadership work?

2. What's your current level of competence in each of the critical leadership dialogue phases?

• Challenging

• Coaching

• Confronting

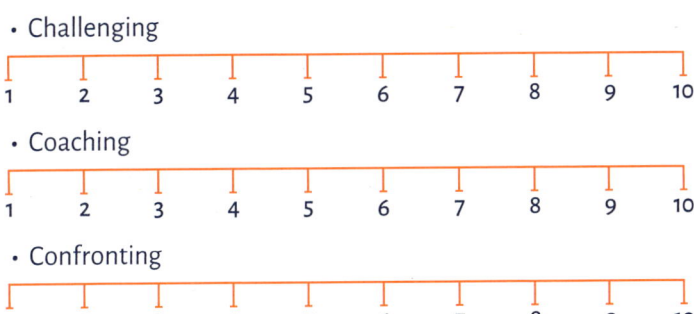

3. To what extent do you formally track your daily habits?

4. How well have you impressed your expectations upon your current team, in terms of each of the following:

• Tone

• Pace

• Standard

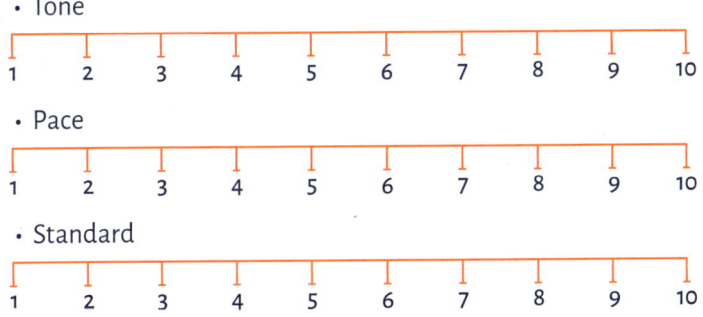

5. How do you rate your current team against the high-performing teams criteria?

6. How highly do you rate your desire to become a no bullshit leader?

CONCLUSION

We all have the capability to change, grow, and improve. While the debate about whether leaders are born or made continues to rage, my lifetime of observation has led me to the conclusion that *anyone* can become a better leader. You can immediately improve your leadership confidence and capability by dedicating yourself every day to doing the practical things that make a difference.

In his book *Talent Is Overrated: What Really Separates World-Class Performers from Everybody Else,* Geoff Colvin explores the role of deliberate practice in attaining mastery in any field. This concept can be applied as readily to leadership as it can to sports and the arts. The key difference with leadership is that most of the practice actually happens in the real-life, day-to-day situations you face. There's no dress rehearsal.

Colvin postulates that there are a number of elements that need to be present for any practice to be considered *deliberate*.

First and foremost, deliberate practice has to be thought out carefully, and designed to create value. The NO BULLSH!T LEADERSHIP framework does precisely that—it identifies the things you should work on if you want to rapidly improve your leadership capability and confidence.

Another key element of deliberate practice is repetition. Like learning to ski in powder snow, sometimes you just have to do something enough times that it begins to feel comfortable. Difficult conversations fall squarely into this category—it's only the first hundred or so that are hard. Eventually they'll feel comfortable.

Deliberate practice also requires independent feedback and evaluation of your progress. Undertaking a 360-degree review process enables you to receive feedback from the people around you, which can be an invaluable aid for self-awareness. You could hire a coach or mentor to work with you, but they only get to hear about your performance as you reflect it to them through *your* lens. A trusted advisor is even better—if you have one on your team, they'll see things that a mentor isn't there to observe. And if your boss gives you feedback, don't succumb to the temptation of dismissing it—she has a pretty good vantage point from which to observe your performance and behavior.

One of the most interesting elements of deliberate practice is that sometimes it isn't fun. And that's OK. If you can push yourself to do things that sometimes make you feel bored, anxious, or even fearful, you're doing what most others won't. As Frank Shorter, the 1972 Olympic gold medalist, said, "You don't run 26 miles at five minutes a mile on good looks and a secret recipe."

Most leaders just go through the motions, repeating their bad habits and mistakes and hoping that will somehow lead to improvement. They'll never attain mastery. If you want to be different, you'll need to commit to doing things differently.

If you dedicate yourself to practicing the leadership methods laid out in this book, your leadership capability *will* improve—and with it your confidence, self-esteem, and job satisfaction. Your people will be happier and more fulfilled in their work, and the results will speak for themselves. //

POST-PANDEMIC LEADERSHIP

The COVID-19 pandemic is undoubtedly the most significant challenge we've faced in our generation. It's gratifying to see how well the NO BULLSH!T LEADERSHIP framework stands up against this backdrop.

I've been developing the framework for many years, and first released it to market as an online leadership program at the beginning of 2019, a year before coronavirus took hold of the world. I started writing this book before the pandemic hit, and I watched it unfold each day across the planet as I wrote.

When it comes to building resilience and mastering ambiguity, there's never been a better time to put these timeless leadership principles to the test. The challenge for you is to ask yourself one very important question: *Do I close my eyes and hope that this will all pass soon and everything will return to normal, or do I find new ways of working and leading in the post-pandemic world?*

No Bullsh!t Leaders will do the latter.

One thing is certain—there will be another major crisis at some point. The world is increasingly complex and interconnected, physically, socially, and economically. Although this brings incredible benefits and potential to the vast majority of humanity, we also need to accept that it comes with some serious downside risks—and many unimagined risks of our interconnectedness have played out graphically during the pandemic.

As the world recovers through the next decade and beyond, don't lose the lessons from the pandemic. Seize the opportunity to build your resilience and change the way you define yourself as a leader. Use this book as your road map, and make the changes permanent. The post-pandemic world will require strong leadership. Weak leadership simply won't cut it.

Even as I write these words, at what appears to be the midpoint of the pandemic, we can already see some emerging trends. There are four in particular that I'd like to briefly touch upon.

| Speed of Change
If we were to examine the millions of disaster recovery

and business continuity plans that organizations had when COVID-19 hit, I'm convinced that none of them predicted the impacts of this event. *Government lockdowns that stop you from trading? Not being allowed to come to the office? Borders closed and international air travel suspended?* But most organizations coped.

What would historically have taken months or even years to achieve was done in a matter of days or weeks. Yes, it was ugly. Yes, shortcuts were taken. Yes, more work will be needed to consolidate these changes. But if this crisis proved anything, it's that most things can be done much faster than we typically choose to do them.

If you need any further encouragement to increase the speed of your decision-making in the post-pandemic world, I can't help you—we've already shown how it can be done. So how do you ensure that you don't regress, but rather embrace the new opportunities this brings?

| Flexibility of Strategy

We've seen retailers moving confidently into online sales, and restaurants moving from dine-in to take-out. We've seen global supply chains severely disrupted, exposing risks that we didn't know existed. We've seen some of our fundamental civil liberties challenged. And we've gotten through it.

The ability to constantly scan the horizon for strategic shifts is now critical for every firm's survival. What may have previously been considered a nice-to-have is now an essential survival skill.

Leading in the future will require a better grip on a world that we didn't think could become any more volatile, uncertain, complex, and ambiguous. It's more important than ever that you learn to sit comfortably in this ambiguity, and make sense of it so that you can communicate your purpose, strategy, and tactics to your people in a rational and compelling way.

Decentralization of the Workforce

Learning to lead people who aren't in your physical proximity is a big shift. It moves you from an input focus (*How much time are my people spending at their desks?*) to an outcome focus (*What are my people actually delivering?*). This shift to outcomes is an important catalyst for value creation.

Pre-pandemic, this might have been a stretch goal for many leaders. But the pandemic has now made it an imperative.

The trend of workforce decentralization will push you a little closer toward a single-minded approach to value creation, however value is defined in your context. It's also likely to shift you emphatically away from any command/control mentality you may still harbor—long-term value can't be created with such an unsophisticated approach.

Technology Penetration

I once jumped on a plane and flew 32 hours from Brisbane, Australia, to London, England, for a meeting—and then flew home. *One* meeting. Of course, the meeting was extremely important, but would I do that today? Probably not—it would more likely be a Zoom call.

Our comfort with using technology as a replacement for face-to-face meetings will continue to grow post-pandemic. We need to be careful, though—working remotely is no panacea. Although CFOs might rub their hands together at the prospect of the cost savings, we need to understand what we might forgo.

Collaboration will no doubt be more difficult to foster, as people aren't having the dozens of corridor conversations that take place in a normal day at the office. Attention spans on video conference calls are shorter, and the ability to engage all participants in the conversation is harder. How do you maintain the quality of decision-making inputs when it's more difficult to get people to put their views on the table?

Innovation may suffer, unless it's deliberately designed into organizational processes. Remote working tends to push leaders more toward task orientation, and the ability to think about the future can be hampered by the many competing demands of the home office environment. Spouses, children, and pets all demand more attention when you're under the same roof.

In terms of the talent pipeline, it'll be much more difficult to spot the potential leadership talent of the future when you aren't constantly in the same physical space as your people. If you can't spot potential talent, it's virtually impossible to nurture and develop it using traditional methods.

Your basic leadership toolkit requires even more compassion, connection, and empathy today if you're to build the level of trust that allows you to challenge, coach, and confront effectively. Replacing face-to-face human interactions with a technology equivalent makes this harder, which means you have to be even more skilled.

Even with these emerging trends, you'll find that the tools you now have are more than enough to help you to cope. Knowing how to *make great decisions, handle conflict,* and paint a bullseye on the things that *deliver the most value* will be rewarded in multiples. Being comfortable *working at the level* you're paid to work at, and giving your people the *accountability* and empowerment to work at theirs will bind your team together, even when you aren't all in the same zip code. And having the *grace under pressure* that all exceptional leaders demonstrate will set you apart in a world that's becoming increasingly difficult to navigate.

LEADING WITH CHARACTER

To finish, let's return to where we started. I promised that this book wouldn't fall into the same traps as most popular guidance on leadership. Although the incredible volume of conventional leadership wisdom is generally true, it's not particularly useful. NO BULLSH!T LEADERSHIP delivers a practical guide to improving your leadership capability and confidence immediately, and well into the future.

People will continue to talk and write about desirable leadership attributes, for the same reasons they've done so over the last 10 years—this kind of aspirational talk inspires, motivates, and comforts you without ever really challenging you to *change* anything.

Humility, fallibility, empathy, transparency, integrity…all of these are incredibly valuable attributes for a leader to have. But on their own, without the deliberate application of strong leadership action, these aspirations fall on fallow soil.

If you assiduously apply the NO BULLSH!T LEADERSHIP framework tools, over time you'll discover a practical path to developing those desirable leadership attributes in yourself. But developing those characteristics isn't easy or quick, which is why most people never reach those lofty goals.

If you can learn to make faster decisions, and to embrace the ambiguity we increasingly face, you'll no doubt make some mistakes. When you make enough mistakes, you'll naturally become more humble. You'll also come to realize that most mistakes aren't fatal, which will bolster your confidence. The ideal complement to humility is *confidence*, not *timidity*—and this makes all the difference to how you lead.

If you embed the *excellence over perfection* philosophy into your culture, you'll ultimately become more comfortable with your own fallibility. Getting things *roughly* right and visibly increasing organizational momentum will unlock untold value. Once you've experienced that, being fallible isn't quite so scary.

Having empathy for others comes from consistently putting yourself in their shoes, and imagining the situation from their perspective. Asking NO BULLSH!T LEADERSHIP questions of yourself and others helps you to understand them better, and to relate more closely. Just remember that the goal is to be friendly, not friends.

Learning to face conflict rather than avoiding it will help you to become more transparent. Instead of hiding the things you should say, you make a point of communicating them in a respectful but uncompromising way. Facing conflict will also make you more courageous, a quality that seems to be declining in today's leaders.

As your courage increases, so does your integrity. You eventually find that you're less afraid of the potential consequences that might come from doing the right thing. Instead, you learn to do what's right, simply because it's right—and you do it when it needs to be done, without hesitating or agonizing over the implications.

Ultimately, taking these deliberate, consistent actions, which are now readily accessible to you in the NO BULLSH!T LEADERSHIP framework, will help you to foster the aspirational leadership attributes that seem so elusive. And, collectively, these attributes combine to become your character.

New England Patriots coach Bill Belichick once said, "Talent sets the floor, character sets the ceiling."

It's up to you now to take this forward and set a new ceiling for your career by developing the character of a no bullshit leader.

ACKNOWLEDGEMENTS

To the people who made this book possible:

My wife, Kathleen Flood Moore, for her unwavering love, support, and belief in me.

My daughter and business partner, Emma Green, the driving force of my life's work, who convinced me that it was a good idea to give up my CEO career and make a real difference in the world.

My daughter Olivia Taylor Moore, for inspiring me to look at the world from a different perspective.

My son, Blake Sbrana, for showing me what real determination and resilience look like.

My mentor, Nick Morgan, and his team at Public Words, who have expertly guided me every step of the way, and without whom these words would never have made it into print.

My agent, Jim Levine, for taking a chance on an unpublished author, and for his experience, support, and belief in this project.

My publisher, Arthur Klebanoff and RosettaBooks, for taking this work on with a level of enthusiasm and gusto that most authors only dream of.

My resident leadership gurus, Brigid Gibson and Danny Hovey, whose expertise and insight I continue to rely upon.

My manuscript editor, Ms. Sarah Morgan, for making this book a much easier read than it otherwise would have been.

The many leaders whom I've learned from, and all the people who made me look good!

Most importantly, our NO BULLSH!T LEADERSHIP podcast audience, students, and clients, whose support and encouragement gave me the confidence to write this book.

EXTRA RESOURCES

SPEAK

Book Martin to speak at your next event.
Visit **martingmoore.com/speaking**
for availability.

LISTEN

For a weekly dose of free leadership content,
subscribe to the **NO BULLSH!T LEADERSHIP Podcast.**

LEVEL UP

Join Martin's 7-week online leadership program,
Leadership Beyond the Theory
at **yourceomentor.com**